Keys to Unlocking Home Ownership

# HOME BUYING
# SECRETS

REVEALED!

Kenn Renner

*Home Buying Secrets Revealed*

ISBN-13:978-1477661550
ISBN-10:1477661557

# What People Are Saying About *Home Buying Secrets Revealed*

"Home Buying Secrets Revealed provides not only knowledge but also many tools to help you make decisions. It gave me some 'ah-ha' moments. For example, the 'Need & Want' list was very helpful. It covers the psychological consoling for a home buyer and we found it very important. 'Buyer Remorse' cost us the first house we made an offer on, but with this book, knowing it is common and what to expect, we felt a lot better with our recent purchase. I would recommend this book to all home buyers, you won't be disappointed."

**Muzi Yu**
**HR Generalist Advisor**
**Dell | Human Resources**

"Thanks to Kenn and his book we were able to grasp the American Dream. Kenn's book took the frustrations and fright out of the equation and made our home buying experience easy and even fun! It shows that Kenn has poured his years of experience and insights into his book. Don't buy a home without it!"

**Geroge & Sylvia Cabello**
**First Time Home Buyers**

"Buying your first home can be an exhilarating experience *and* incredibly intimidating at the same time. Kenn's easy to read book takes the mystery out of the process with a straightforward, step by step approach covering everything from what to look for in the home itself to nailing down the financing. I know you'll love it."

**Rob Hutton**
**President, DR Horton Homes, Central Texas Division**

"Buying a home is probably the scariest thing I could have ever thought of doing. *Home Buying Secrets Revealed* helped prepare us for what we went through. While it never happens the way you expect and there are always bumps in the road, having a good Realtor and the right information made the bumps a little easier. It's the most rewarding thing ever to walk in your home knowing it's all yours!!"

**Ron & Mellissa Kammburger**
**First Time Home Buyers**

"*Home Buying Secrets Revealed* is a must-read for anyone considering buying a home. Kenn is a master strategist and communicator and delivers a compelling, comprehensive and concise guide to home buying. From building credit to mortgages to building a team of professionals – Kenn covers it all in this very timely, informative, entertaining and easy to read book."

**Dr. Bruce Cook**
**Venture Capitalist**

"I found Kenn's book to be well though out, very informative, and educational. It was also very easy to understand and an excellent tool for anyone looking to buy their first home. Kenn's history as a mortgage professional as well as an expert in the real estate market only adds to the viability of this book. I also love the personal touch and empathy contained in this work, especially the story of Kenn buying his own first home."

**Kenton K. Brown**
**Vice President, Sente Mortgage**

"I finally have the 'go to' book for my first time home buyers to read."

**David McMillan**
**Host of Real Estate Radio, KLBJ-590 AM**

# Table of Contents

# Top Ten Home Buying
# F.A.Q.s and Answers

F.A.Q. #1 – "Is real estate a bad investment?"

Answer #1 – "Buying the right home at the right time is always a good investment."

For the past several years, we have been inundated with "bad news" about real estate. Values dropping, foreclosures at all time highs. Doom and gloom. The media thrives on bad news and rarely reports even a silver lining about housing. The truth is that buying the right home at the right time is <u>always</u> a good move. Savvy investors who are rich (and I would not include most of the media makers in that category) buy <u>low</u> and sell <u>high</u>. The smart investors and home buyers "buy" in a buyer's market – not a seller's market. Unfortunately, first time home buyers are most vulnerable to media influence and become fearful at the very time they should be bold and step into the market when others are hesitating. I have witnessed buyer's markets turn to seller's markets within a six month time frame. Real estate is cyclical and will always be so. The good news is home values historically increase over time. Be careful not to listen to real estate bashing friends and co-workers. Sometimes even well meaning, sincere relatives can give poor advice when it comes to real estate and where values are headed. You may hear "Don't you remember uncle John lost his shirt in real estate in the 1980s," or "Aren't you fearful of the foreclosure crisis – right now is not a good time to buy?!" Don't listen to hearsay – get the facts! Do what the rich do and buy <u>low</u>!

Donald Trump was recently interviewed by a pessimistic news media pundit setting up a question to Mr. Trump with a string of bad news statistics about real estate and home values. Donald Trump answered quickly with "Yes! And the great deals are everywhere!" Being able to buy low with low cost of money – now that is the sound of opportunity ringing.

**Secret Revealed: There are only a few places you can store wealth and real estate (including your home) is one of them.** (See Chapter Two – Home Buying – Reasons Why.)

F.A.Q. #2 – "Can I afford a home?"

Answer #2 – "It can cost you more <u>not</u> to buy a home."

Many first time home buyers think that they can't afford to buy a home. The truth is that in many cases, a first time home buyer can't afford to continue to pay rent. In fact, a buyer's market combined with low interest rates combined with government income tax incentives can make purchasing a first home the ideal financial and lifestyle move. As the saying goes "you have to live somewhere." The question is – where are you going to be investing your monthly housing dollars – in <u>your</u> future or in your landlord's retirement? You pay for where you live, so why not invest in your own home rather than some one else's. With all the great deals in the housing market it is possible to buy a home with a ton of equity (value) already built-in. If you ask any of your parents or older relatives if they were glad they purchased their first home, they would probably say they wish they had purchased it sooner than they did. They would also probably say it was one of their best financial moves they ever made.

Rent payments can go on forever but a home will eventually be paid off. Then you will own the home "free and clear" with no mortgage payment – forever. Furthermore, rent is not tax deductible whereas a home payment is almost completely tax deductible off of your income. Why not make the IRS pay a portion of your living expenses? When you know the facts, you may realize you can't afford to keep paying rent.

**Secret Revealed: Renters make landlords rich because of tax breaks, equity build up and loan principle buy-down. These are all the same reasons why you should consider ownership rather than renting.** (See Chapter Two – Home Buying – Reasons Why.)

F.A.Q. #3 – "How can I come up with the money to buy a home?"

Answer #3 – "Money to purchase a home can easily be found if you diligently look for it and ask for it."

Source of funds to purchase a home is a common concern for first timers. Many first timers overestimate the actual amount it will take to purchase a home and underestimate the readily available sources of funds to close. The most popular first time home buyer program is F.H.A. (Federal Housing Administration). F.H.A. is a government insured loan that requires as little as 3.5% of the sales price as down payment. Veterans can obtain a V.A. insured loan that requires a 0% down payment. Other zero down loans such as U.S.D.A. programs are available in many areas. There are additional closing costs and expenses that are associated with buying a home and sellers are allowed to pay some or all of these expenses. When you make an offer to purchase you will have to negotiate with the seller to help cover your costs. So a 0-3.5% down payment with the seller or builder paying closing costs can get you into a home.

Other common sources of funds to close can be government bond money offered by state and local municipalities. Gifts from non-profit agencies and charitable organizations can be used. Gifts from relatives or friends are common. You'd be surprised who wants to help you with the purchase of a home if you would just ask. Believe it or not, the mortgage lender and even the real estate professional can contribute towards your funds to purchase the home. Most employers will allow employees to borrow from their 401k for the purchase of a home. I.R.A.s can be tapped into up to a certain amount without penalty. How about the sale of that boat or other personal asset that you have sitting around. One of my clients sold a horse to come up with the funds to help buy a home. You will be amazed at how many possible sources there are once you start asking and looking. One important point: make sure you document your source of funds very well. Your mortgage professional will require all your funds to be documented with a "paper trail."

**Secret Revealed: Uncovering sources of funds to purchase a home is like a treasure hunt. The funds are everywhere you just have to find them.** (See Chapter Seven – Home Loan Secrets.)

F.A.Q. #4 – "I heard the banks aren't lending money for homes?"

Answer #4 – "Banks and mortgage companies are ready, willing and able to lend money for homes."

Media spin doctors continue to report more falsehoods regarding the reality of the mortgage market. The truth is that there is no shortage of funds and banks & mortgage companies are eager to lend it out. Just think, the money we put in a savings account earning 1%-2% or less and can be lent by the banks at 5-6% to home buyers! That is a huge spread. The banks enjoy making money on that spread by lending it out on government backed home loans. Not to mention the loan fees that are generated when funding a home loan. Yes, guidelines have tightened but more akin to the guidelines we had before "sub prime" was ever a household name.

The government has been encouraging banks and mortgage companies to lend. The F.H.A. (Federal Housing Administration) insures more than 25% of new home mortgages originated in America. More than 50% of first timers are F.H.A. insured. F.H.A. loans offer low down payments (3.5% down) low interest rates, and easier qualifying. There are even zero down loans still available and government grant money available for down payment assistance in many counties. The truth is a home buyer with marginal to good credit with a small down payment and a source of income (a J.O.B.) can qualify for a home loan – all day long!

**Secret Revealed: Banks and mortgages companies need to lend money – it's their business. To stay in business they need to lend money to home buyers like you.** (See Chapter Seven – Home Loan Secrets.)

F.A.Q. #5 – "Do I have to have great credit to buy a home?"

Answer #5 – "Homebuyers with marginal credit can still qualify for F.H.A. financing."

Yes – your credit score is more important than ever. Not only will your score affect your ability to get a car loan, a credit card, or a home mortgage –it can affect your insurance rates and even employment possibilities. The problem is most people don't know their score. In fact, the score can change daily so who can keep up? With all that's riding on the credit score, it is in our best interest to find out what the score is and learn what to do to raise it. Most lenders want to see a credit score of 640 or above to fund an F.H.A. loan. The average score in the United States is around 660 so a person with below average credit scores can still qualify for a mortgage. The prudent thing to do is to apply for a home loan with a trusted reputable lender and within minutes, you will know your score. Often times, the score is perfectly acceptable to get a home loan. Sometimes the score is just below the cut-off and a home buyer may only need to do a few minor things to get the score up to acceptable levels.

The truth is that there are a few very simple techniques and strategies you can use to increase your credit score. Of course, paying on time is a given. Keeping balances low in ratio to the credit limit is a huge factor, so sometimes simply moving some balances around may be advised. Make sure NOT to close active charge accounts that you have had for a long time.

There are things you may think would raise your score but will actually lower it. For instance – paying off old collection accounts can adversely affect your score (and cost you money unnecessarily). So it is a good idea to find out what will help raise a score and what will lower a score, and then act accordingly.

**Secret Revealed: You can get your score for free and you can manipulate your score if you know what to do and what not to do.** (See Chapter Six – Credit Report Secrets.)

F.A.Q. #6 – "I don't think I need a real estate broker. Can I really trust them anyway?"

Answer #6 – "A trusted, experienced real estate professional is your indispensible counselor and administrator who guides you into your home."

It amazes me how the next generation of home buyers don't feel they need the help of a real estate professional. The truth is that buyers (especially first timers) need the help of a real estate professional more than anyone. First of all, the inventory is controlled and represented by seller's agents. The job of a seller's agent and a builder's onsite representative is to get the seller/builder the most money and the best terms. Many buyers have the notion that they can locate, negotiate, and work through the process of home buying without the professional help on their side. What a shame and what a mistake. The fee for the buyer's representation is built into the listing agreement between the seller and the seller's broker. The seller's broker will pay a commission to any buyer's agent that brings a buyer who buys the home. Not only that, the buyer will have a professional negotiator and administrator to help them each step of the way. Let me repeat. The fee for the buyer's exclusive representation is already paid for by the seller. The buyer pays nothing for this service.

As far as trust – a recent Harris poll showed that real estate professionals were ranked in the top "3" of least trusted professionals. The stereotype is that real estate professionals are perceived as sales people rather than educated consultants. Part of that stereotype is true. Many real estate professionals are not perceived to be as educated as say doctors or lawyers. But the reality is that an educated, trusted real estate professional is indispensable to the home buying process. Your goal should be to find and hire (at no cost to you) a trusted buyer's representative to guide you through the home buying experience.

**Secret Revealed: Top real estate professionals save you a ton of time, effort and money and can put you in a much better negotiating position than "going it alone."** (See Chapter Four – Trusted Advisors.)

F.A.Q. #7 – "Can I save money by buying directly from the seller/builder because they won't have to pay a buyer's agent?"

Answer #7 – "An effective buyer's agent's responsibility is to get the buyer the best possible price & terms and their fee is already agreed to and paid for by the seller/builder."

I've heard it over and over in my twenty-five plus years of selling homes. Home buyers (especially first timers) think that if they buy a home directly from the seller or builder they should get a better deal because the seller won't have to pay a buyer's agent's commission. So they should get a better deal, right? "Au contraire" my friend. The commission agreement is between the seller and the seller's broker. The seller's agent "agrees" to share the commission with the buyer's agent. The seller's agent is not obligated to pay a home buyer any portion of the commission. In fact, the fee that would have been paid to the buyer's agent for the buyer's representation is kept by the seller's agent if the buyer doesn't have his own agent. Do you think a seller's agent who is obligated to the seller AND who is going to make a double commission if there is no buyer's agent is going to encourage a buyer to get his own real estate professional? Not likely.

This rookie mistake also happens with new homes. Buyers who deal directly with a highly trained on-site sales representative will most likely not be getting a better deal and certainly will not have exclusive representation. Buyers think they will "get a better deal" if they don't have a buyer's agent –

WRONG! Buyer's agents level the playing field with builders and on-site sales representatives. Buyers agents also know which builders are good, great, and not so good. Not only do they know which ones are good, bad, or ok, they also know which communities are better than others. Builders highly value a buyer's agent because they can continually bring new buyers to their communities. As I say to my clients, "You may only buy one house from this builder in a lifetime but I may bring them a dozen buyers in the next year. The builder has a stake in keeping both you and me happy because it could mean a lot of future business to them." Once again, the builder pays the fee for the buyer's representation and they won't reduce the price if you don't have a buyer's broker. If a builder did lower the price by the commission – the real estate agents would stop bringing their clients to that builder for fear of being "cut out."

You shouldn't go to court without representation. You don't go to an IRS audit without representation. Why would you make one of your biggest lifetime investments without your own representation – especially since the seller/builder is paying the fee?! Don't make this rookie mistake! My advice to you – get representation. It's already paid for!

**Secret Revealed: A buyer's agent can get you the best deal on the right home and their services don't cost you a dime.** (See Chapter 5 – Step 3 – Consult.)

F.A.Q. #8 – "With the internet, don't I have access to all the info I need to make a prudent home buying decision?"

Answer #8 – "The internet is a great source of real estate information but you need an experienced real estate professional if you want wisdom."

As wonderful a resource the internet is for real estate and for home buyers, it still lacks the professional human element of <u>wisdom</u> that can make for a successful property search and smooth transaction. Home buyers can learn a lot about neighborhoods, homes, schools, employers, and traffic on the internet, etc. But the information on the internet is incomplete and can be misleading. For instance, a common mistake I have observed is home buyers getting home values from the tax records. Yes, the tax records can be found on the county assessor's website, but those values can be off by 10% or even as much as 20% or more in some cases. Many of the big name property search engines like "Zillow" for the most part use tax assessor values to give their guesstimates of value. Once again, these values can be outdated or flat out wrong. Real estate appraisers and real estate professionals use "sold" comparable properties called "comps" that have closed in the past six months to extrapolate value. They make adjustments based on size, condition, amenities and usually come up with a much more accurate market value for a home. "Sold" data is not readily available to the consumer via the internet yet. So, only those real estate professionals who have membership to the local MLS (Multiple Listing Service) will have the "sold" info including property condition and seller concessions (discounts). Also, real estate professionals have much more information at their disposal about home values, trends, and important facts about an area or a particular home. If you contact the listing agent (seller's representative) you will get the basic facts but not the insight and perspective that your own exclusive representative will bring to the table.

A home purchase is one of the biggest financial moves anyone can make. To trust the internet's limited and sometime wrong information is asking for trouble. Finding a trusted real estate professional with a team of advisors at their disposal is much more advisable than "going it alone" or relying on blogs or internet websites for wisdom.

**Secret Revealed: Top internet real estate websites are run by tech-savvy pros but not necessarily the best qualified real estate professionals. The best agents are found by referral.** (See Chapter 5 – Step Five – Find Property.)

F.A.Q. #9 – "Can I find the lowest rate home loan on the internet?"

Answer #9 – "You should not be shopping for the best interest rates. You should be shopping for the best loan professional."

Once again, the internet can be a very useful tool when researching home loans. Most lending internet sites are designed to capture your contact info so you can be solicited to. Once again, as great as the internet is for information it still lacks the human element of wisdom.

One big mistake I see is homebuyers "shopping" for interest rates on the internet. You may "think" you are getting the lowest rate and fees only to find you are duped with a bait and switch. It happens all the time. There are a lot of unprofessional lenders out there that can make your home buying experience a nightmare and they are often the ones that dupe unsuspecting "shoppers" with the "lowest rate." The truth is if you shop the very lowest interest rate, you'll probably end up working with a flake.

The lending business is a competitive, complicated and an ever-changing market. Not only do interest rates fluctuate on a daily basis, but so do lending requirements and guidelines. You need to find a trusted lending professional who keeps up with the changes in rates and terms. Someone who can explain the programs and costs associated with a home loan. Someone who will present the best possible loan programs to fit your particular lifestyle and need. You want a loan professional that will walk you through the process from beginning to end.

Because of the attrition in the lending business, longevity is a factor. You want to deal with a full-time lending professional who has three to five years or more in the business. Lending professionals and loan companies come and go so you want to deal with ones with a proven, stable track record.

Here is a true story about what can happen if you just shop rates on the internet. I had a client who had "found" the best rate on a home loan on the internet. Knowing what I know about offers on the internet I researched the company. They had a nice looking, professional website. I Google mapped the address for the business and found the address to be an apartment building in another city. Further, I checked the loan company's status with the state agency that regulated loan companies and found out they had lost their license to make home loans. Needless to say, we passed on this lender and we went with a local, reputable loan professional who got them a very competitive rate and who walked them through the loan process. The loan professional even showed up at the closing and explained the various loan documents they were signing. You won't get that kind of service from an out of area "internet" lender.

**Secret Revealed: Internet mortgage websites give you information but not the wisdom and service you need. The best lending pros are found by referral.** (See Chapter 5 – Step Four – Apply For Financing.)

F.A.Q. #10 – "What if I am stuck in a lease?"

Answer #10 – "You shouldn't let a lease keep you from buying the right home for you and your family."

Time after time, I see homebuyers miss out on great opportunities to buy the perfect home because they feel they are "stuck in a lease." You should not let a lease obligation get in the way of you buying a home that is right for you and your family. There are several ways to approach the issue. Your real estate professional or your attorney can help you. The first thing you have to do is pull out the lease agreement and see what it says. This is a good practice anyway because reviewing your lease may also reveal other obligations that you may have committed to. For instance, many leases now require a 60-day notice. You may "think" you only need to give a 30-day notice, but what is in the lease is what stands.

Review your lease agreement and see what your legal obligation is and see what your worst case scenario might be. Sometimes the worst case is "no big deal." Typically, when you sign a lease, you are obligated to pay the entire amount of the money owed for the entire lease period. In some cases, there is an "out" if you pay a penalty – which can be a lot less than paying the entire remainder of the lease. I have experienced many times when tenants found out that they could get out of their lease and buy a home for just a small fee to their apartment complex. Believe it or not, your landlord may even let you out of the lease at no cost if they can rent the property for more than you were paying. Another strategy – simply ask the landlord about your wanting to move and would they let you out of the lease obligation. Sometimes a landlord's situation has changed and maybe they have decided to sell the property and would be glad to let you out of the lease so they can market the home for sale. You may ask them to allow you to replace yourselves by finding a friend or co-worker to "take over" your lease. I have even seen where tenants have advertised on Craigslist that they have a potential property for lease, found a suitable replacement tenant, and presented them to the landlord. The landlord was thrilled that their property would not become vacant. Then there is negotiation. You may approach a stubborn landlord and offer them a "settlement." A sum of money that will make them willing to let you off the hook if you paid it up front, cash on the barrel. This often times can be attractive to the landlord because they may be able to get the property leased again right away and come out ahead.

Finally, ask your real estate professionals if they will help out. Many realtors, builders, and sellers may be willing to help out through "lease buy out" programs and other assistance to "get you out of your lease." Don't let a lease get in the way of you buying the right home! Check out www.MoveAssistancePrograms.Com for more helpful ideas.

**Secret Revealed: You don't have to let a lease keep you from buying the right home. There are win-win strategies you can**

**use to "tell your landlord goodbye."** (See Chapter Five – Step Two – Make a plan.)

## A Note about QR Codes and Bitly Shortened URLs

Throughout this book you will see the following symbols (known as QR codes) and shortened URLs that lead to videos of me discussing the sections of the book. Feel free to use your smart phone to scan in the QR code or type the Bitly URL into your web browser to unlock additional content. These videos will also be frequently updated with additional information well after the printing of this book. The first one appears below and relates to this FAQ section.

Watch Video
http://bit.ly/NvPA6G

# Secrets Revealed Recap

1. There are only a few places you can store wealth and real estate (including your home) is one of them.

2. Renters make landlords rich because of tax breaks, equity build up and loan principle buy-down. These are all the same reasons why you should consider ownership rather than renting.

3. Uncovering sources of funds to purchase a home is like a treasure hunt. The funds are everywhere you just have to find them.

4. Banks and mortgage companies need to lend money – it's their business. To stay in business they need to lend money to home buyers like you.

5. You can get your score for free and you can manipulate your score if you know what to do and what not to do.

6. Top real estate professionals save you a ton of time, effort and money and can put you in a much better negotiating position that "going it alone."

7. A buyer's agent can get you the best deal on the right home and their services don't cost you a dime.

8. Top internet real estate websites are run by tech-savvy pros but not necessarily the best qualified real estate professionals. The best agents are found by referral.

9. Internet mortgage websites give you information but not the wisdom and service you need. The best lending pros are found by referral.

10. You don't have to let a lease keep you from buying the right home. There are win-win strategies you can use to "tell your landlord goodbye."

# Introduction

## My First Home Buying Experience – Anchorage, Alaska, 1983

It was fall of 1980 when my father & I moved to the Great White North. I had spent most of my life growing up in Southern California and my dad had moved to Alaska to pursue his dream of becoming a real estate developer after a decades long career as a corporate real estate attorney. Ever since he first read *The Call of the Wild* by Jack London, his dream was to live the pioneering life in Alaska. During his years as an attorney with a large oil and gas company, he had made many business trips to Alaska for his company.  In researching the economy of Alaska, he recognized the boom/bust nature of its oil-based economy. He researched the exodus of population after the completion of the Alaska pipeline and the subsequent drop in real estate values. There was a real estate market pattern that he predicted would continue. He was right. The Alaska economy started recovering. My dad gathered investors together and began buying bargain apartment buildings and renovating them. As the economy began to boom again, those apartments filled up, rents increased and things were looking good.

**SECRET REVEALED – Real estate markets are cyclical.**

I graduated from high school at East Anchorage High School. After high school, I went to work at a grocery store. I remember the manager (who was in his mid 50s) saying to me that if I worked hard and continued on a grocery store career path I would be able to become a retail manager just like him. Fortunately, I did not share his same passion for shopping baskets and long hours at the cash register.

So I decided to go to work for a professional property management firm. I was eighteen years old and glad to be out of the parking lot pushing grocery carts in sub-zero weather. The property management company managed condominium homeowner associations. I received my first experience in community management. Not a very glorious job, but it was a living and paid the bills as well as gave me a steady enough income to qualify for – you guessed it – a home mortgage loan! At the time, I also studied for and acquired my first real estate license and at the age of nineteen, I became the youngest person in the state to earn a real estate license.

During Alaska's booming early 1980s economy, my sister was an on-site sales representative for one of the large tract homebuilders in Anchorage. She eyed a particularly nice lot at the end of a cul-de-sac. A very unique lot that she knew would be a winner. She approached me and asked if I would like to buy a home with her. I thought long and hard – for a few minutes and then agreed and said, "Sure, let's buy a home." So we began the process. Needless to say, my youthful exuberance soon turned to fear when I considered the enormity of buying a home. The thirty-year payment commitment – "come on" – thirty years? I was nineteen and looking at being forty-nine before it would be paid off.

**SECRET REVEALED – Buying your first home may seem like an enormous endeavor, but it's really not.**

That's a long time. What if I lost my job? What if I did not want to live in Alaska any more? What if? What if? It was a classic case of buyer's remorse. Still, I moved forward with the commitment and the home buying process, questioning myself and those involved – suspicious of who was asking me for personal information.

**SECRET REVEALED – Credit glitches are common and can be overcome.**

I met with the mortgage loan officer in a high-rise glass building where she took my personal information and had me sign what seemed like an endless stack of fine print documents. She was going to run my credit, which I knew would torpedo this whole process and send me back to my apartment, defeated and a failure. I knew she'd find out about that gas card that, a few years earlier, I "forgot" to pay until they took it away. (Hey, it was either pay the bill or pay for pizza.) Needless to say, I knew I would be openly ridiculed by her "discovery" of my past gas card transgressions. Still haunted by the enormity of the thirty-year mortgage, I signed the loan paperwork to get started and get my pre-approval so the builder could start building the home. Nervously, I signed everything and threw my personal credit history and my modest income at the mercy of the mortgage company's court of opinion. The mortgage loan manager looked at me and saw my pre-determined discouragement and assured me with a smile, "everything is going to be ok – you qualify for the loan, your sister is co-signing with you and a simple letter of explanation is all that will be required for that gas card slip-up a few years ago." "Really?" I said. "Whew, not so bad after all. Hey, thanks. And you work in a pretty nice office too. I'd like to do what you do some day." As I walked out of the office, seeing busy loan processors and people hard at work on their paperwork and running to make copies, I thought, "I really would like to do this kind of work some day."

**SECRET REVEALED – Even today, mortgages are easier to obtain than most people think.**

**SECRET REVEALED – Every home buyer will experience buyer's remorse at least once during the process and must push through it.**

Over the course of a few months, my little home off of Muldoon Road in North east Anchorage was built. I was able to pick the colors of the carpet and cabinets and it was fun to see the home "come to life." As the home neared completion, the enormity of my home buying endeavor started to creep back into my psyche. I was revisiting "buyer's remorse." On a cold winter day, I was led to the title company to sign the final papers. I was paralyzed with the fear of commitment. I remember sitting at the closing table, not wanting to sign, then refusing to sign. My sister placed the pen in my hand (she knew it was a great deal) encouraging me. "Come on, you can do it little brother," she'd say. I said, "Ok, Ok. I'll sign my life away."

**SECRET REVEALED – The day you own a home for the first time is exhilarating.**

After that, I went to my new home and went, "Wooohoo! I own a house. This one's my baby!" What a sense of accomplishment with the help of my family and some nice professionals along the way. I was the new owner of my own $75,000 piece of Alaska!

Well, things were going great until a few months later my family started to make plans to move back to "the lower forty-eight." I was thinking, "Great, I just bought a home and now everyone is going back to California without me." What was I going to do? Fortunately, my sister came to the rescue. She had sold the home across the street from me to a retired marine. His lifelong marine buddy was retiring also. They had served together in two wars and were the best of friends. Their dream was to live next door to each other in retirement. But my house was the one he wanted (I had the nicest lot thanks to my sis). To him, this particular house was not about the cost, it was about living the rest of his years next to his best buddy. So he offered us $103,000 for the home I was living in (I had only owned it six months!).

**SECRET REVEALED – Buying a first home can be a great investment.**

Yippy! Sold! My sister and I netted over $25,000 on my first home and I was free to head back to "the lower forty-eight" with the rest of my family. All the fear, the trepidation, the mysterious process with signatures in high-rise buildings all came to an end with an enormous profit and a win-win for all involved. What a cool deal, now "this" is first time home buying.

**SECRET REVEALED – A free and clear home can make retirement much easier.**

Even more interesting was that the ex-marine was paying cash. He explained that he had grown up in the depression and paying cash was how he liked to do business. I thought to myself, "Wow, a home with no mortgage payment, that would be nice. What a comforting thought in his retirement, to not have to worry about a big debt."

Looking back, I have to agree with him. If I had kept the little home I had in Alaska, it would have now been paid off and I would own it "free and clear." I could rent it out and enjoy the income or have it as a second home where I could visit Alaska any time and have a place to stay or offer it to friends and family. I could even have used it as a retirement home – paid for.

**SECRET REVEALED – A free and clear first home can be a great investment or vacation home.**

This experience lead me to a career path that has enabled me to assist literally thousands of first time home buyers through the process of purchasing a home. I have taught seminars nationwide on the subject of homeownership and investment. I still get a huge thrill assisting first timers through the process. I also enjoy teaching them all the ins and outs, giving them money saving tips and advice. I also love to uncover the secrets that I have learned over my twenty-five year career that can help them save time, effort, and money as well as keep them out of trouble and help them avoid costly mistakes. I also encourage them to think about keeping their first home when they move on as an investment or retirement home. No one ever forgets their first time home buying experience and I want to encourage those who are thinking about it to get prepared with proper planning and finding trusted professionals, then moving forward.

**SECRET REVEALED – First time home buying seminars are a great way to learn the process and meet real estate professionals.**

I now have the pleasure of assisting second-generation first timers buy their homes. Clients who purchased their homes with me over the years are encouraging their children to call me to help them through the process.

It has also been my pleasure to help my industry associates in real estate learn how to best assist first time home buyers through educational classes and forums. I thank you for taking the time to read this book and I guarantee it will answer questions and save you time, effort, and money. Join me now as we uncover the secrets to buying your first home.

**SECRET REVEALED – Connect with knowledgeable real estate professionals with experience and who love what they do.**

Watch Video
http://bit.ly/JZwyzH

# Secrets Revealed Recap

1. Real estate markets are cyclical.

2. Buying your first home may seem like an enormous endeavor but it's really not.

3. Credit glitches are common and can be overcome.

4. Even today, mortgages are easier to obtain than most people think.

5. Every home buyer will experience buyer's remorse at least once during the process and must push through it.

6. The day you own a home for the first time is exhilarating.

7. Buying a first home can be a great investment.

8. A free and clear home can make retirement much easier.

9. A free and clear first home can be a great investment or vacation home.

10. First time home buying seminars are a great way to learn the process and meet real estate professionals.

11. Connect with knowledgeable real estate professionals with experience and who love what they do.

## Section I – Home Buying Motivations

# Chapter 1

## The Great American Dream

It has been called "the Great American Dream." The right to own your own home, to have deed and title to a property that you can call "your own." A place where you live and spend most of your time. Where you raise a family. Where you gather with loved ones for celebrations and holidays. A place where you do life together. A place of refuge from the "world." A place where memories are made. The word "home" invokes deep emotions of security and connectedness. "Home is where the heart is."

Home ownership is a key component of the American value system, and is at the core of the American lifestyle. Providing shelter for both ourselves and our stuff but also providing a shelter for our financial future when treated properly. The truth is we all have to live somewhere and the choice is simple. We either rent or we own. Approximately 68% of Americans own their own home. The other 32% rent. Historically one third of Americans either should rent or are forced to rent. Depending on the circumstances and timing, renting can be an advisable alternative to owning. Although in the long term, the benefits of home ownership almost always outstrip those of renting. The fact remains – you can rent forever until your last days but a home can be paid off. One day a home loan will be paid in full and you will own your home completely "free and clear" – debt free.

Your first home might very well be the best home for you to keep for your retirement. Although I myself never plan to "retire," the reality is that some day I may not want to or be able to work. That little one story home I purchased in Alaska so long ago would be paid for and waiting for me if I ever had the need to live there, debt free. The reality is that a majority of baby boomers and "boomerangs" are not planning for the ultimate time when they don't want to or can't work any more. Simply keeping your very first home as a place of free and clear living could be the best "secret" I share with you in this book.

**SECRET REVEALED: Keeping your first home may be your best retirement home.**

## The Perfect Storm into the Perfect Opportunity

At the time of this writing, the Nation is in the midst of a tough economic recovery. The recession was in no small part created by the perfect storm caused by over inflated home prices driven by sub-prime easy mortgage money. From the early 2000s to '05 and '06, there was an unprecedented run up of home prices driven by easy qualifier financing and sub-prime loans that had thrown out sensible lending criteria because of a seemingly unlimited supply of funds. The basic lending foundations of borrowers needing to be required to have income, assets, and a history of repayment seemed to vanish and stupid loan after stupid loan was funded. The largest Ponzi scheme in history came to an end with dramatic measures – government interventions and trillion dollar bailouts.

The lending guidelines that were so loose just a few years earlier became very tight – exacerbating the problem and

2

delaying recovery because ready, willing and able buyers were being kept out of the market, not able to buy the assets (foreclosed homes) that were causing the problems.

# Media Mania

Ahh, and then you have the ever present media driving fear and uncertainty into the hearts of Americans. Nothing like a dose of bad news blast after bad news blast to keep people from doing what they can and should do to get the economy moving. Bad news feeds into the public psyche and it paralyzes the buying decisions of those that needed to and should be buying. The media spin-doctors compounded the problem because "if it bleeds, it leads." Bad news sells. If you were not "Chicken Little" then just watch the newscasts long enough and you too will start exclaiming, "the sky is falling." The good news is that no one has gotten rich watching the news and furthermore, if you are getting your financial wisdom from newscasters, you may very well end up unhappy, depressed, and broke.

**SECRET REVEALED: Don't get your wisdom from the news media.**

The news media is full of half-truths and flat out lies. All of this "perfect storm" real estate news of the real estate "sky is falling" is music to the ears of the shrewd and prudent. As Donald Trump said in a recent interview, "the deals are everywhere." That's right! The best time to buy is – when? In a buyer's market. When should you buy? When sellers are scared (from watching too much T.V.) and they want to give you their home, their fridge, their motorcycles – all at bargain prices.

**SECRET REVEALED: Buy in a buyer's market.**

I have heard many newscasters (big national ones) talk about the "fact" that no one can get a home mortgage. That lending has "shut down" unless you have a 20% down payment and stellar credit – Lies! The Federal Housing Administration –

has stepped up and is insuring hundreds of thousands of home loans with just a 3.5% down payment – all day long. Don't believe too much of what you've heard on T.V. or in the newspaper or you might live your life in a mentally sub-prime mode.

# The Perfect Opportunity

The three factors that make first time home buying the perfect opportunity are –
1.  Government subsidized low interest rates
2.  Government home buying incentives
3.  Buyer's market

# Cheap Money!

If you had told me a few years ago that interest rates would be under 5% I would have thought you might be a bit looney. But here we are with the lowest interest rates in history allowing you to buy more house with less monthly obligation than ever before. And even if rates go up, it is still cheap money. Furthermore, the cheap money is tax deductible. That's right – the low interest you are paying on a home is a tax write off. In other words, the government pays a portion of your home payment.

**SECRET REVEALED: Because home payments are tax deductible, the government is partially subsidizing your home payment.**

The low rates and the tax deduction make it the cheapest money you can borrow. And you are borrowing it to buy a place you can live in and enjoy. When the economy starts to improve, interest rates will start going up. At that time, you will pay more money for less house. Don't wait too long. If rates go up it means inflation is coming back, which means that the value of hard assets – like houses – will also go up. It is simple economics. Low cost of money spells "opportunity."

**SECRET REVEALED: When interest rates go up, the value of assets (homes) usually follow.**

## Government Programs & Incentives

The government understands the economic impact of first time home buying. From local municipalities to state & federal government, leaders have been coming up with programs to help consumers become home owners. Everything from tax credits to down payments assistance, to bond programs that make home ownership more affordable.

The Federal Housing Administration (F.H.A.), Veterans Administration (V.A.) and even the U.S. Department of Agriculture (U.S.D.A.) have programs to get buyers in to homes with little or no money down at today's very low interest rates.

These loans are not the same ugly loan types that got us into trouble a few years ago. You still need a source of documentable income. Your credit scores can't be in the gutter. You have to have a measure of stability. The government is subsidizing your purchasing of an asset that you get to use, live in, and enjoy for as long as you wish. No one complains about a bigger tax refund. Why not enjoy a subsidized home payment? The saying goes "you have to live somewhere, why not have Uncle Sam help out?" It's the American thing to do.

**SECRET REVEALED: The government wants you to buy a home to help the economy.**

## Buyer's Market

"The prices are falling. The prices are falling." Yes and eventually the prices bottom out and head up again. It's a fact of life. Prices go down and then they go back up again. The problem is that very few ever buy at the very bottom. Prices start going back up while home buyers sit on the fence waiting for a bottom. By the time prices move up they are past the bottom and prices are already going up. The time to buy is in a buyer's market. Ask any savvy (wealthy) business person and they will tell you – "buy when no one else is buying." It seems like a bold move to buy in a buyer's market, but it's a smart move.

The perfect opportunity of cheap money, government subsidies, and a buyer's market are rare occurrences. I encourage you to think hard and plan wisely to take advantage of this rare convergence – this perfect home buying opportunity.

**SECRET REVEALED: Perfect opportunities are rare.**

# Shelter Me!

A few nights ago, a strong line of thunders moved through our Central Texas region. As the rain and the wind whipped around my home, I felt safe and cozy in my warm bed. I thought about one of the biggest reasons for owning my own home. Consider the basic necessities. You know – food, clothing and <u>shelter</u>. As obvious as it sounds, our homes provide one of the basic necessities of life – shelter. Keeping us safe, warm and providing us a place to store all of our necessities.

Our homes are also shelter for our net worth. Even in tougher economic times, much of the average American's net worth is found in the equity in their homes. Homes are a shelter for our financial as well as our personal assets.

Homes also shelter us from income taxes. For most of us, one of the largest debts over our lifetime is the income taxes we pay to the government. The IRS allows us to deduct most of our home payment and property taxes from our income. This provides a tax "shelter" which allows us to use the savings for other necessities or investments.

A recent report by the Federal Reserve Board of Consumer Finance showed the average net worth of a renter to be $4000 and the average net worth of a homeowner to be $184,400. Statistically, you are more likely to have a far higher net worth as a home owner than as a renter. Owning your own home can also shelter you financially in your later years. Think about holding onto your home and paying it off over time. When you retire, one of your largest expenses, your home mortgage, could be completely eliminated.

**SECRET REVEALED: Owning your own home is more than just physical shelter, it can be financial shelter, an income tax shelter and a retirement expense shelter.**

## "Psyched Up" For Home Buying

Although I purchased my first home when I was nineteen years old, most first timers are in their late twenties or early thirties. First timers may have started a family, are thinking of starting a family, or may be simply looking for more stability in their housing situation. First timers are usually out of college and have started their careers. Although I have helped college students purchase their first home while still in school. Such was the case for two brothers who were psychology majors at the University of Texas who bought a four-bedroom home not far from the campus. Even though they didn't have a job, Mom & Dad co-signed with them and they lived for less housing expense than they would living in a dorm. They even rented a couple of rooms out and actually <u>made money</u> on the home that they owned while they went to school. At the time, their home payment was $736 per month. They rented two rooms out for $400 per month each. Wow! Rent-free while going to college. These two psychology students who were first time homebuyers instantly became real estate investors. Buying this home with their parents also helped them establish a credit history. And after four years of college and two years of graduate school, they had an asset that was on its way to being paid off. After they finished school, they could have sold it for a profit, continue to live in it, or rent it out and keep it as a long-term investment property!

**SECRET REVEALED: Buying a home as college housing can be a great move.**

## It's Your "Season"

Whatever the season of life you are in when you purchase a first home – it is an exhilarating and tenuous time as you weave your way through the process. You'll learn new terminology that you've never heard of. You will be inundated with new information and multiple decisions that will affect the outcome. You will be offered advice both good and bad from well-meaning and sometime not-so-well meaning individuals and websites. There will be times of triumph and then times of buyer's remorse. The good news is that with proper guidance and a ready, willing, and able mindset, you will make it to the finish line. You will enjoy that day when you wake up in your new home and realize the satisfaction of knowing that – it is yours. All the hard work, the learning curve, and the expense will all be worth the price when you wake up that first day in your own home!

**SECRET REVEALED: Buying your first home is challenging and exhilarating.**

Watch Video
http://bit.ly/LGE4Vs

## Secrets Revealed Recap

1.  Keeping your first home may be your best retirement home.

2.  Don't get your wisdom from the news media.

3.  Buy in a buyer's market.

4.  Because home payments are tax deductible, the government is partially subsidizing your home payment.

5.  When interest rates go up, the value of assets (homes) usually follow.

6.  Perfect opportunities are rare.

7.  Owning your own home is more than just physical shelter, it can be financial shelter, an income tax shelter and a retirement expense shelter.

8.  Buying a home as college housing can be a great move.

9.  Buying your first home is challenging and exhilarating.

# Chapter 2

## Home Buying – Reasons Why

The three main reasons to become a home owner are security, tax benefits, and investment.

## Security

Owning your own home can be more secure than renting for a number of reasons. Home owners are in more control of their living situation. When you own you are not subject to a lease or a landlord's rules. Leases by design are for a shorter period of time, usually one to two years. Depending on the market, your rental amount will most likely increase. As a landlord myself, I almost always increase my rents at renewal time. When the rental market is really tight, these rent increases can be dramatic. When you own your own home with a fixed rate home loan, your home payment will remain the same over the life of the loan. Your property tax rates and home owner's insurance can vary from time to time, but your mortgage payment will remain the same. With interest rates as low as they are your home payment may even be less than a rent payment. And as you pay down your loan balance, your equity (the difference between the home value and the outstanding loan

11

balance) can increase. Eventually your home will be paid off completely and you will own the home "free and clear." The truth is, you can rent forever but a home mortgage will eventually be paid off. Keep in mind, there are times when leasing is more advantageous than owning. If you are only going to be in the home for a short time, then you may want to consider renting. Home ownership is a medium to long-term investment – three to five years or longer.

**SECRET REVEALED: Your fixed rate home loan will someday be paid off.**

# You Won't Be Forced to Move

As a home owner, you won't be forced to move. When a lease term is up, the landlord has the right to raise the rent or force you to move by not renewing the lease, or the landlord may decide to sell the home. A friend of mine lived in a rental home for six years where she was content. The kids were comfortable with their schools and loved their "home." My friend even did improvements to the home. She put in some built in shelves and planted flowers and a garden. After six years of being a loyal renter, the landlord decided to sell the home. She was forced to move and incurred moving expenses. This disrupted the kids' living situation and she ended up paying substantially more rent at the next home. In hindsight, her better move would have been to buy the home she was living in from the landlord. This can be a great strategic move. I have helped thousands of renters become home owners and one of the easiest ways to become a home owner is to buy the home you are renting (at reasonable price and terms of course).

**SECRET REVEALED: Buying the home you are renting can be a great way to become a home owner.**

# Improvements Are Yours

Another benefit of homeownership is that you have more freedom with the personalization of your home. You can change paint colors, make additions, add wood floors – whatever you want. When you are renting, you have to get permission from the landlord to make these kinds of changes and they usually stay with the property.

**SECRET REVEALED: Home owners are in more control of their housing situations.**

Home ownership provides more stability and more freedom to personalize. Home ownership also provides a stable payment with no rent increases. A home payment can actually be cheaper than a rent payment. With interest rates as low as they are combined with the income tax savings, your next housing expense could very well be less than rent.

**SECRET REVEALED: A home payment can be less than rent.**

# Tax Benefits

Uncle Sam favors home ownership. Your federal government knows the impact of home ownership and encourages it through income tax incentives. Mortgage interest and property taxes are deductible off of your income. There are additional tax-deductible expenses when you purchase a home. For instance, up from distance points (fees paid to lower your interest rate are deductible in the year of your purchase). Other fees associated with the purchase of a home can be deductible. Check with your accountant regarding these additional deductions.

**SECRET REVEALED: Uncle Sam favors home ownership.**

For first timers, the home mortgage interest and property tax deduction will have the most immediate impact as a new home owner. Uncle Sam allows you to deduct home mortgage interest, and property taxes off of your gross income. Most of your home payment is interest and taxes. So for example, if you make $50,000 per year and you have a $1500 house payment (interest & taxes). You would be paying $18,000 per year for your home. Uncle Sam will allow you to take the $18,000 off of your $50,000 gross income and will only tax you on $32,000 in income. Let's say you were in the 25% income tax bracket, you would pay $12,500 in income tax. But because you have an $18,000 home payment deduction off of your income you will only be taxed on $32,000 and only then pay $8000 income tax. This is a savings of $4,500 per year or $375 per month that you will not have to pay the IRS. So a $1500 home payment is actually a $1,125 per month house payment expense after taxes when compared to renting. This is one of the biggest "ah-haaas" I get from my first time clients. They tell me, "I pay $1000 per month in rent. I am comfortable with that as a house payment." I then inform them, "ohh, then you can afford a $1200 per month house payment because you won't be paying as much to the IRS in income taxes." Then they say "wow, that's great, but will I have to wait until next year's tax returns to realize the savings?" I tell them, "no, go to your employer's H.R. department and tell them you are now a home owner and would they please decrease the amount of withholdings from your paycheck." Isn't it great to know that Uncle Sam will be helping you make your home payment!

**SECRET REVEALED: You can ask your employer to withhold less from your paycheck after you buy a home.**

## Home Purchase Expense Deductions

Most first timers don't know that the IRS will allow you to deduct a portion of the home purchase expense. When I go to closing with a home buyer, I point out these expenses and tell the home buyer to give the closing statement to their accountant at tax time because there are tax deductible expenses when you purchase the home. Discount points (fees paid up front to lower the house payment) are tax deductible <u>even if the seller pays the discount points</u>. There are potentially thousands of dollars in income tax deductions available to you just for buying a home!

**SECRET REVEALED: There can be huge tax deductions when your purchase.**

Now, when you go to sell your home, the IRS will not charge you a capital gains tax on any of the profit up to $250k for singles and up to $500k for married couples. You just have to had lived in the home two out of the past five years preceding the sale. This is huge. Think about it. If you were fortunate enough to make $500,000 in profit on your home (if married) it would be tax-free.

**SECRET REVEALED: You can enjoy up to $500,000 tax-free profit on the sale of your home.**

# Investment

The third of the big three reasons to become a home owner is investment. Yes, I know you have been hearing the news on how real estate has tanked and it is not a great investment. Don't believe the news media. Real estate investing over the years has been a major cause of wealth build up for millions of millionaires worldwide. Real estate, including your home, is a medium to long term investment. Dealt with responsibly, your home will probably prove to be one of your best investments ever. The ones who "lost their shirt" in the latest boom & bust cycle were for the most part speculators who timed the market wrong or those who got stuck with a nasty sub-prime loan. As a result, we have all seen the fall out. Foreclosures and bank owned properties flooded the market. Do you know what all this means for a prudent, responsible first time home buyer today? Opportunity! That's right! A buyer's market! I always tell my clients – you make your money on the home when you buy it. And right now you can cherry pick and buy right.

A few years ago, we saw the stock market's Dow Jones drop from 14000 to around 7000. Tell me, when was the time to buy? Yeah, when everyone else was selling. When prices were down, when panic hit the streets. How many of you bought stock when the Dow hit 7000 or less? Hmmm? Same with real estate and your first home. Buy low, with cheap money, (low interest rates) enjoy your tax benefits and enjoy the use of the home, and then watch it appreciate over time. "Appreciation" you say? Yes, appreciation. That's what usually follows a sell off in the market. Granted, no one can guarantee appreciation but over time, home values tend to increase. According to the national association of realtors, the home prices nationwide have increased an average of 4.4% per year for the past twenty-five years. This takes into account booms and busts and is averaged over time. Here again, the key phrase is "over time." If you purchase a $150,000 home and it performs at the national average over the next five years the home could be worth $186,900. If you put the minimum down payment of 3.5% or $5,250, what would your return on that initial investment be. Over 700%. Wow! On an average performing home. Now you have to be wise and informed and the national average over the next few years may change. But if you buy at a deep enough discount – who cares? You made your money by buying right.

**SECRET REVEALED: More people have become wealthy by owning real estate than by other investments.**

Watch Video
http://bit.ly/LQOUEv

# Secrets Revealed Recap

1. Your fixed rate home loan payments will someday be paid off.

2. Buying the home you are renting can be a great way to become a home owner.

3. Home owners are in more control of their housing situations.

4. A home payment can be less than rent.

5. Uncle Sam favors home ownership.

6. You can ask your employer to withhold less from your paycheck after you buy a home.

7. There can be huge tax deductions when you purchase.

8. You can enjoy up to $500,000 tax-free profit on the sale of your home.

9. More people have become wealthy by owning real estate than by other investments.

# Chapter 3

## My "Rich Dad / Poor Dad" Story

I am sure you have heard of or have read Robert Kyosaki's classic book *Rich Dad, Poor Dad*. It's the story of Robert's "two dads." One who was conservative and worked his whole life to earn his money – his "Poor Dad" – and the other, his "Rich dad," who made his money work for him. I have my own true-to-life "Rich Dad, Poor Dad" story that will bring home the advantages of owning real estate over time (especially your first home).

My earliest memories were in the first home my father had purchased in the early 1960s. My dad was just coming out of the army. He was a lawyer and was beginning his civil career as a corporate attorney. The home was located in San Mateo, a quiet suburb of San Francisco, California. He purchased the nice little one-story ranch style home on Lexington Lane for $17,000 and had a payment of just $144 per month. He bought the home with a VA (Veteran's Administration) zero down loan.

After we lived there for several years, he was relocated by his company back East and we moved. My father then sold the home for $28,000. This was the first real estate he had owned which he bought using a zero down V.A. loan. He made a profit of over $10,000 which he thought was a pretty nice gain – and it was. But he would have done "much" better had he held on to it – more on that later.

**Secret Revealed: You can still buy a home with no money down!**

# I Coulda – I Wish I Woulda

Through the years, we moved to several different homes, some of which he bought and sold and some of which he rented. But because my dad never kept any of the homes he owned for the long term, he never built lasting wealth from real estate, nor was he able to shelter his corporate income from Uncle Sam while renting.

During the latter years of his life he ended up living on Social Security which you and I know is not enough to live on. When he ran low on money, I was fortunate enough to be able to cover his apartment rent for several years until he couldn't take care of himself anymore and moved to the "old folks home" where he lived out the rest of his time. It was an honor to help my beloved dad during his latter years but life for him could have been much different because of just one house.

I can't help but think back to that first home where I had my first memories and imagined what his life would have been like if he had kept his first home. When we moved back East, what if he had put a renter in the home that would have paid the $144 per month over the remaining years left on the home loan? The home would have easily been paid off – free and clear – in the early 1990s. For the last fifteen years of his life, he could have lived debt free in the quaint one story home in San Mateo "or" he could have collected rent from the home at about $2000 per month (the current going rate) and had a nice supplemental income in his retirement years. What if? What if? Just that one home paid off would have made his life so much easier.

**SECRET REVEALED: One free and clear home can make retirement much easier.**

# My Rich Dad

Recently, I had lunch with my father-in-law who is a real estate agent and investor. He currently is enjoying his semi-retirement, playing with the grandkids, traveling the country and working on his rental properties. We talked about the first home he owned. It was a three bedroom, two bath home located on Marathon Street in San Diego, California. It was 1150 square feet and he purchased it for $15,900. His payments were $139 per month. In three years, he sold this home and took the profits and rolled it into a 2500 square foot home on Pisces Way for $27,900. He then sold that home and with the profits, he had a $40,000 home built in Fountain Valley, a suburb of Los Angeles. This home he kept for over twenty years. He then sold it for $485,000 and moved to Austin, Texas.

I asked him if he wished he had kept his first house. He exclaimed "Oh Yeah! You're darn right I wished I kept it!" It's worth over $500,000 today even in the slow San Diego real estate market. In fact, he wished he had kept all three of his first homes. However, he was fortunate that each home afforded him the opportunity to purchase more homes and investment properties in different cities. He was able to pull cash out of the homes through refinancing over the years and use the cash as down payments on rental property. Over the years, he was able to build up a portfolio of real estate which would put him in the "wealthy" category. So even though he had sold his first home (which he wishes he still had kept) he was able to collect property after property with the help of the equity from his primary homes and others. He still can't forget that if he had just kept his first home that he paid $15,900 for so many years ago that he would have had an extra half million dollars to play with today!

**SECRET REVEALED: Most everyone wishes they had kept**

**their first home – myself included – hindsight is 20/20!**

# The Accidental Millionaire

The reality of my "Rich Dad, Poor Dad" experience is that real estate over time will be paid off and historically increases in value. Yes, there are down times in the market (and that is the time to buy!), but over the long haul, home values increase. Looking back at the home my conservative dad purchased in San Mateo in the early 1960s for $17,000, that home today is worth in excess of $1 million. And that value is down 20% from the peak of $1.2 million just a few years ago. That one home would have been paid off – free and clear – over fifteen years ago it would have made my dad a millionaire. Just for holding on to it and paying it off! He would have been an "accidental millionaire." Not only that, he could have lived well off of the equity through a reverse mortgage during his latter years.

I did an exercise and counted up the current value of homes that we had lived in over the years while growing up, whether we rented or owned, and calculated the current net value of those homes. Even through economic booms and busts, the values of those homes today would be over $5 million. Furthermore, those homes would have been paid for – free and clear by now! Simply buying, holding, and paying off residential homes that we get to enjoy the use of is one of the easiest and most sure ways to become an "accidental millionaire."

**SECRET REVEALED: While one free and clear home can make life easier, ten free and clear homes can make you wealthy.**

Watch Video
http://bit.ly/LRrZLA

## Secrets Revealed Recap

1. You can still buy a home with no money down!

2. One free and clear home can make retirement much easier.

3. Most everyone wishes they had kept their first home – myself included – hindsight is 20/20!

4. While one free and clear home can make life easier, ten free and clear homes can make you wealthy.

**Chapter 4**

# Build a Team of Trusted Advisors

## The T.R.U.S.T. Factor

Buying a first home will probably be the biggest financial move you will make up to this point in your life. It is not something to take lightly. It is a serious move and you will need help. The good news is that there are teams of trusted advisors and professionals who are available to assist and guide you into your new home. These advisors will be on your side. The really good news is that these professionals' fees for their services can be paid for by others or as part of the sales price of the home. It amazes me how many times home buyers forego the help that is available to them. The cost of this help is an almost pre-paid investment and is already covered in the price of the home. For instance, most real estate agent fees are usually paid by the seller or builder. The mortgage company and title & escrow fees can be included in the sales price or paid by the seller. Your goal should be to find these trusted professionals and employ (deploy) them. But you need to make sure these professionals work for you and not anyone else.

You wouldn't make a major medical move without your trusted physician. You wouldn't make a major legal move without your trusted counsel. You shouldn't make a major financial move like purchasing a house without a trusted advisor. Better yet, a team of advisors who work for you.

**SECRET REVEALED: As a first time home buyer, you can easily build a team of professionals who work exclusively for you.**

A recent Harris poll reported that real estate agents are in the top three "least" trusted professions. The good news is that there are plenty of professionals that you can trust. You need to track them down, get a hold of them and don't let them go. They can become your trusted professionals for life and they tend to associate with other trusted professionals that you may also have access to.

The team of trusted professionals that can help you achieve your goal of home ownership may also lead you to key lifelong business relationships that can help you to succeed in many other future endeavors. Find an established, trusted advisor who has other advisors that they are "networked" or "tethered" to. I call this professional a "key" advisor. This person can be a real estate professional, a mortgage lender, a family attorney, financial planner, insurance broker, or a CPA. They are well established and well connected. They usually have <u>more than five years of experience</u> in their business and are well respected by their peers. Believe me, you can find them. Maybe the person who gave this book to you is a key professional. Keep asking around and you will find trusted advisors. Your goal is to hire a team of trusted experts who will advise you, mentor you, and have your best interests in mind.

**SECRET REVEALED: T.E.A.M. stands for Trusted Experts, Advisors, & Mentors.**

# T.R.U.S.T.

## "T" is for "Truth"

The T in Trust stands for a foundation of Truth. Your mutually beneficial relationships begin with your trusted professional having the utmost integrity. And you must be truthful with your professional. Your advisor needs you to be honest about your wants, needs, and motivation.

**SECRET REVEALED: Integrity is the foundation of trusted relationships.**

## "R" is for "Respect"

Your professional needs to be experienced, trained, strategic, a skillful negotiator, likeable, available, and trustworthy. Your trusted professional must respect you and your objectives. The biggest complaint I hear from clients about other professionals is "they didn't listen to what I was saying or what I wanted." Expect the highest level of care, communication, and competency. I call these the three "C's." The unfortunate fact is that first time home buyers are perceived by many in the real estate industry as low R.O.I (return on investment) for the real estate professional. This is an unfortunate mistake made by industry professionals because if a first timer is treated well, educated well, and respected by their professional, they become a raving fan referring friends, family, and co-workers any chance they get.

**SECRET REVEALED: Ask for and expect care, communication & competency.**

## "U" is for "Understanding"

The U in T.R.U.S.T. stands for understanding. Your real estate professional must understand your objectives. The professional must consult with you to discover your needs and wants as well as what you don't want in a home. The real estate professional must understand your buying style. Some buyers make quick decisions and don't want to look at a lot of houses – just the best homes that fit their criteria. They are ready, willing, and able to make a decision today. Other buyers are more methodical. They will take their time when looking for homes. Let your professional know how you like to buy. An understanding of buying style will minimize frustrations and accomplish your objective much more effectively. You need to understand your professional's position as well. Do they have the time and availability to work with you? You may be able to locate the best professional in town, but if they are too busy or unavailable, find another one (or ask them to refer you to another professional who is in the "excellent" category).

## "S" is for "Security"

The fourth level of a trusted relationship is security. You want to get to the level of trust where your real estate professional can be your confidant. A secure relationship is one where you can share your deeper desires and motivations. You are able to discuss private matters like credit, bank balances, family situations, dreams, and ambitions. A secure relationship is one where you know that personal information will be safe with them. I have a financial planner and a CPA that I feel safe in giving them my most important personal information. If you don't feel secure with your real estate professional, you won't refer them to your friends and relatives. A real long-term mutually beneficial business relationship comes from the trust level of "security."

## "T" is for "Tethering"

Tethering is the fifth level of T.R.U.S.T. This is where there is so much mutual trust that you will figuratively tie yourself to your professional and they will tie themselves to you. Think of a mountain climbing expedition. The professional is your lead guide and when the going gets steep, they tie their rope to you. Now that's trust. Tethering also means you are ready and willing to throw the rope out to your friends, relatives, and co-workers. In other words, you will refer your real estate professional any chance you get. The lifeblood of the professional sales business is referrals from satisfied clients and former clients. You are seeking a professional that you can trust so much you are willing to refer them at all times. You become a raving fan. When you ask people you trust who they employed to do the job look for the "raving fan" reaction. "Oh, you really need to meet my real estate professional. He did a great job." "You need to talk with my mortgage lender. She is awesome!" Likewise, your real estate professional should have a network of trusted professionals that they will connect you with. They throw their "lines" out to their team of proven trusted professionals – lenders, inspectors, builders, insurance agents, etc. Trusted advisors love to refer loyal clients to their network. This is the lifeblood of the professional's business – either direct referrals from a client or a referral from another trusted advisor.

**SECRET REVEALED: True professionals seek to turn their clients into raving fans.**

# Be Referred

There is a higher level of accountability and responsibility to a referred client as opposed to someone who calls off of a classified or internet advertisement. For the professional, there is a greater R.O.I. (return on investment) because the "referred" client has a certain level of implied trust already. Real estate professionals love to refer other professionals. When I refer my clients to my trusted mortgage professionals, they get priority service. Why? Because my mortgage professional may get a dozen or two dozen clients referred to him by me every year. They value my referral – big time.

My clients will often come to me and ask about agents in other cities. If you are planning on moving out of town to a different city, let your in-town real estate professional refer you to an agent in the next city. They have an obligation to find you the best professional in that city. There is an accountability factor, not only to you but to the referring agent as well. Your in town agent gets a small percentage of the out of town agent's fee – so it's a win-win for all involved.

**SECRET REVEALED: If at all possible, refer and be referred.**

## Win-Win Accountability

It is common in other professions to be referred. For instance, if you go to your trusted family doctor and he/she said that you need a specialized procedure, your doctor will "refer" you to the best specialist in town. This specialist will give you favor because you have been referred by another professional. Your doctor may refer dozens of clients a year to the same specialist. The specialist wants to keep this flow of business going by making sure the patient – you – has a good experience. You will report back to your doctor your good experience and that will encourage your doctor to keep sending patients to that specialist. If a bad report comes back to your family doctor about this specialist then your doctor may call up and find out why you had a bad experience and may even cut off the referrals to that specialist if the problems continue. The same scenario happens in real estate and their network of professionals. If I send a client to a lender, I expect that client to get top-notch service and professionalism. If my buyer reports back a "bad" experience, I will get involved. The lender has accountability to you the buyer *and* to me the referrer.

Watch Video
http://bit.ly/KyEeum

# Secrets Revealed Recap

1. As a first time home buyer, you can easily build a team of professionals who work exclusively for you.

2. T.E.A.M. stands for Trusted Experts, Advisors, & Mentors.

3. Integrity is the foundation of trusted relationships.

4. Ask for and expect care, communication & competency.

5. True professionals seek to turn their clients into raving fans.

6. If at all possible, refer and be referred.

# Section II – Making Home Ownership Happen

# Chapter 5

## The Ten Steps to the Home Buying Process

### Step One – Decide

Step one in the home buying process is to make the decision to become a homeowner. Make the decision, commit to it, take action, and then – never give up. If you are serious about purchasing a home and are patient and persistent, you <u>will</u> be able to accomplish the objective of home ownership. I have helped a multitude of homebuyers become homeowners who never thought they could become one. I have helped a client buy a home in one week from start to finish. I have also worked with a client for over three years to get them into their first home. As long as you are committed and willing to work through the challenges, rest assured you can get that first home. Credit need not be a problem as long as you are willing to take the steps to establish or re-establish your credit rating. Cash need not be a problem if you are willing to budget and/or seek available down payment assistance or other sources. The important thing is to make homeownership a <u>goal</u>, <u>write it down</u>, <u>commit to it</u>, and then take the proper action steps. For some it will be easy. For some it will be a challenge. But everyone who is willing to take the steps and work through the process can enjoy the American Dream of homeownership. I have helped thousands of renters become homeowners and the ten steps we go through are the same for everyone. Each transaction is unique, but the basic steps are the same. I also teach goal achieving courses and have found that those who know how to write down their goals in detail and then are willing to take purposeful, planned action every day are much more likely to achieve results quicker and easier than those who don't. Make the decision, commit to it, take action, and then – never give up.

**SECRET REVEALED: Make homeownership a goal, commit, take action, and never give up.**

# Your (First) Dream Home

Take some time and dream a little dream of your first home. And then dream a big dream of your ultimate dream home. The place you start to get to your dream home often starts with your first home. My first home in Anchorage, Alaska was a two bedroom just under 1,100 square feet. It was my first "dream home." My current home was an ultimate "dream home" in my mind years ago. Now it's my family's "reality home." So take a look into the future and visualize your ultimate dream home. Then take a look into the near future and visualize your first home.

**SECRET REVEALED: Visualize yourself in your own "dream" home.**

# Real Estate is Still About Relationships

A majority of first time home buyers are in their late twenties and early thirties. The current trend is that the emerging generation appears to be buying their first homes earlier. The current generation of first timers tend to be internet savvy, prefer texting over voice mail, and are a little suspicious of the real estate professionals and home builders. They like to do their own research and look for homes via the Internet. They will usually get information up front and then start to move into the buying decision mode. They tend to not engage a real estate or mortgage professional until they are further along in the process. They will often depend on their tech savvy first and on professionals later. This can be good and bad. What first timers should seek first is a trusted advisor or team of trusted professionals that they depend on and use tech skills to enhance these relationships. First timers without professional guidance can make uninformed decisions or talk themselves out of buying a home completely. It is easy to make an unwise home choice based on their Internet searches. Real estate is still very much a people and relationship business, so in making a decision and a goal to purchase a home – make aligning with the right professionals one of your first priorities.

**SECRET REVEALED: Real estate is still a people and relationship business.**

# Don't Listen to Nay Sayers

If you have decided to make homeownership your goal, don't listen to those who don't share your enthusiasm. There are plenty of voices out there that will tell you what a bad idea buying a home is. They could be co-workers, "friends," family, a blog, or newscasters (or those listening to "the news"). If buying a first home is your goal – avoid listening to them or keep your home buying goal secret from them. Align with those who share your enthusiasm and who will encourage you. Talk with those who believe in real estate and who own their own homes.

Believe it or not, most nay sayers are going to be people who don't own their own homes.

**SECRET REVEALED: Stay away from nay sayers who don't own their own home.**

So in review:

A) Decide
B) Commit
C) Make it a Goal
D) Take Action
E) Align with the Right Professionals
F) Stay Away from Nay Sayers
G) Never Give Up

For more information on how to set and achieve goals visit: www.GoalsSeminar.com.

## **Secrets Revealed Recap**

1. Make homeownership a goal, commit, take action, and never give up.

2. Visualize yourself in your own "dream" home.

3. Real estate is still a people and relationship business.

4. Stay away from nay sayers who don't own their own home.

# Step Two – Make a Plan

Step two in the home buying process after having made the decision, is to make a plan. Planning involves self-analysis and determination. Determine the end result and then make a commitment to get there. You will want this plan with you when you meet with your trusted advisors because your plan will become more defined and refined with their counsel. Making a plan will set the groundwork for you to become "ready, willing, and able" to buy a home. You will need to analyze your readiness, your willingness, and your ability to purchase a home.

**SECRET REVEALED: Make a plan to become "ready, willing, and able."**

# Do a Self-Analysis

First, start with an honest self-analysis of where you are. Look at your current lifestyle and think about your future living style. Where are you at personally? Are you single? Getting married? Planning a family? Getting a divorce? Where are you relationally? Who will be living with you? Who will be involved in the home purchase decision? If there are others involved in the home buying decision, a significant other or a parent, you will probably need to include them in the analysis. Make sure all decision makers are involved in planning. If your parents or anyone else will be involved in helping you buy a home, make sure they are involved from the beginning.

Next, do a self-analysis of your finances and your budget. How much rent are you paying now? What are your other monthly expenses? How much do you think you can afford in a home payment? How much per month is comfortable, how much would be a stretch? Putting a budget together will help you see where you are at.

Are you planning a job change or a move to a different location? What do you enjoy doing for recreation? What is really important to you in your lifestyle? Is being close to a gym important? Do you want to be able to walk to shopping or a coffee shop? What kind of commute to work is ideal? How long of a commute is too long? Make a list of what's really important to you. Rank the list on a scale of 1-10 with 10 being the highest.

**SECRET REVEALED: Self-analyze what is really important in your preferred living situation.**

# Ready & Willing

Now ask yourself and your home buying partner (if you have one) "If we could accomplish a majority of our objectives, would we be ready to move forward?" If the answer is yes then you have stepped into the next phase – willingness.

I have known people who were "ready" for years but until they become willing, nothing happens. Willingness means you start taking action steps toward purchasing the home. If you can answer the question "If we found the right home in a reasonable period of time, with acceptable payment, and terms, would we buy it?" If the answer is "yes" then you are ready & willing home buyers. Start taking action steps. When you are ready and willing, you need to track down trusted advisors because they will help you become "able."

# Able

You may be ready and willing, but are you "able?" This often needs to be worked through with your trusted advisors. Sure, if you won the lottery and have cash and know where and what you want to buy, then go for it. The rest of us will need to work through the process that includes a team of professionals who will help you with your home buying plans. If you need help with cash, you can find it. If you need help with credit, you can find it. Help is available.

## Needs & Wants List

During the preliminary planning stage, I like to have my clients start a needs and wants list for their first home. I recommend they take out a piece of paper and put a line down the middle. On the left side, I tell them to put "needs" and on the right, I have them put "wants." At the bottom of the page, on the right, I put another small box titled "don't wants."

I then have them write down their needs in their next home. Needs are "must haves." Needs are minimum requirements like "I need at least three bedrooms and a two car garage. I need a minimum of 1500 square feet." The needs can also include maximums as well. "I need a payment of $1200 per month or less or no more than a thirty minute commute to work." I once sold a first time home to a baby doctor who had to be no more than fifteen minutes from the hospital because of deliveries. This was a "need." What are your "needs" – write them down.

Then on the right side, you will list your wants. These are "It would be nice to haves." They are not absolute requirements, but "nice to haves." "It'd be nice to have a pool" or "It'd be nice to have a media room." Then I recommend listing don't wants on the bottom right. Like "I don't want to live on a busy street" or "I don't want a big yard to take care of" etc.

**SECRET REVEALED: A needs and wants list will help clarify objectives.**

## Ranking Your Needs & Wants

I then recommend ranking the needs and wants on a scale of 1-10 in importance with 10 being the most important. Everyone has different needs and wants. I sometimes find that after doing this exercise husbands and wives have different opinions on the value of the needs and wants. Doing this ahead of time will help everyone involved and may save you from some awkward moments. Then of course, rank your don't wants.

# Timing

Part of planning is timing. When do you want to be in your home? If you are going to buy a resale home you will need to start the process ninety days or more in advance of when you want to move. Even if you are ready, willing, and able, it may take you one to three weeks or longer to find your home and then another forty-five to sixty days to go through the purchase process. This is not a rule, just typical. What my team of experts has been noticing is that the total time frame for today's home buyers from deciding to action is longer than it has been in the past. The time from when some one becomes interested in buying a home to actually making a decision and moving forward is longer. Maybe this is just a sign of the times – home buyers being more cautious and not anxious, or maybe the younger generation of home buyers are more methodical, in no particular hurry, and suspicious of real estate professionals. Whatever the reason, the time from "interested" to "deciding and taking action" is longer than in the past.

**SECRET REVEALED: If you are buying a resale home, start 90+ days before you want to move.**

If you are planning on building your first home with a home builder, the time frame is substantially longer. The build times for even a small single family home can be five to six months. So when you add the planning and searching time, you are looking at beginning the process up to <u>nine months or more in advance</u>. If you are not sure if you are going to build or buy a resale home, then you need to consider the longer time frame of nine months. You can always adjust your time down if you decide that building from scratch is not in the cards. This is why when a potential client says they just signed a new one-year lease, I tell them that we need to start home buying planning soon because if they decide to build, they will need the extra time to search for the location and go through the building process.

**SECRET REVEALED: If you plan to build, start the process nine months before you plan to move.**

# What about Your Lease

The timing associated with your lease is always a factor. If you are planning to buy a home it would be best to go on a month-to-month rental, even if the month-to-month rental rate is higher. Even better is to get a lease with an option to leave early at no penalty with thirty or sixty days notice. This way you won't be forced to move out of a month-to-month earlier than you want to. If you are in a lease and you feel stuck, take a look at the lease agreement. Some leases will let you out with notice and a small penalty like 80% of one month's rent. Some lease agreements are more stringent and require you to pay all the lease amount owed for the entire time left on the lease. This often stops buyers from moving forward with home buying plans and can cost them missed opportunities. I tell my clients not to let a lease get in the way of buying a home. They might miss a great buy on a great home or interest rates could rise costing them way more over the long haul. There are ways to work around your lease. One way is to simply ask the landlord if you can get out. I have helped clients on several occasions get out of a lease by simply approaching the landlord and politely asking for permission to move early. You can also offer to the landlord that you will help find another tenant to replace yourself and take over your lease. Some leases allow subleasing where you can lease to someone else at the same rate and terms that you had. You can run an ad on Craigslist or post a flyer at work.

Another way to get out of a lease is to offer the landlord a cash settlement. In a strong market, the landlord may just take two or three months up front rent to break out of a lease. Ask your real estate professional. At times they are willing to help you with breaking your lease or even help cover some of the cost of breaking the lease.

For more helpful ideas visit:
www.MoveAssistancePrograms.com.

**SECRET REVEALED: Don't let a lease stand in the way of you buying a home.**

# How Long Do You Plan on Living in Your Next Home?

Another important consideration in timing is how long do you plan on being in your next home? If you are buying your first home, it will probably be three to five years or longer. If at all possible, I recommend that my first timers consider purchasing their second house first. I see first timers often buy a first home that is just right for their current needs and lifestyle. They quickly outgrow the little home and come back in a few years and have me find them a bigger home. If they had bought the bigger home first, they would not need to go through the time, effort, and expense of a move so soon. They would get more living years out of the bigger home. This is not to say to push yourself out of your budget, but to just consider it as an option. If you just got married and plan on starting a family, you will quickly outgrow a one bedroom/one bath condo. Consider a bigger home the first time if it makes sense for your future needs.

**SECRET REVEALED: Consider buying your second home first.**

# Secrets Revealed Recap

1. Make a plan to become "ready, willing, and able."

2. Self-analyze what is really important in your preferred living situation.

3. A needs and wants list will help clarify objectives.

4. If you are buying a resale home, start 90+ days before you want to move.

5. If you plan to build, start the process nine months before you plan to move.

6. Don't let a lease stand in the way of you buying a home.

7. **Consider buying your second home first.**

# Step Three – Consult

After you have made the decision to buy a home and have a preliminary plan, a budget, and a needs & wants list, the next step is to consult with trusted advisor professionals who will help you through the process. This is a very important step. If you miss it, you may end up making choices you later regret. So often I hear of home buyers who got excited about buying a home that they ran out to the first subdivision they could find and ended up buying a home that was not the one they really needed. Or they see a sign in a yard and buy the home from the seller's agent and end up not getting the fair deal that they deserved. You can avoid this by taking a little time and gathering the professionals together who will work for you to help you through the process rather than dealing with sales people who may not have your best interests in mind.

**SECRET REVEALED: Get excited, then hire trusted advisors.**

The real estate agent (broker) and your lender are on the forefront of coordinating your home purchase. These two professionals will coordinate most of the activities and direct the rest of the personnel through the home buying process. There may be other professionals you need to consult that are not necessarily in the real estate industry. Your attorney if you need legal advice. Your accountant if you need tax advice. But for the most part, your real estate professional and your lender are your key professionals in this process. I realize that first timers don't always have attorneys and CPAs at their disposal but if you need legal or tax advice, you should get it from those qualified to give it.

**SECRET REVEALED: The real estate broker/agent and lender will coordinate 90% of home buying activities.**

# Consultants vs. Sales People

Real estate professionals are perceived by the public as "sales people." It is too bad that my associates are perceived as sales people but it is our industry's own fault. Fortunately, the image is slowly changing by the educational efforts of organizations such as the National Association of Realtors and individual professionals making the effort to improve the industry's image. The good news is that there are real estate professionals that raise the level of professionalism to that of lawyers and doctors. They are experts.

**SECRET REVEALED: There are real estate professional who are "experts." Find them and employ them.**

# Seek Consultants

What you should be looking for in a real estate professional is a consultant – not a salesperson. Consultants have high levels of service and expertise. They ask questions, listen to responses, filter the responses through their years of knowledge and experience and then give informed responses. They will take your individual needs and wants list, refine it, and help you to realize your goal. They will offer suggestions to make things easier for you. You may not be exactly sure what you want or what is realistic. Consultation will help you become clearer about the possibilities and processes. Consultants are great at motivating you through the process towards your next home. Some in the industry on the other hand tend to do a lot more talking and a lot less consulting. What is amazing to me is how few first time home buyers will seek real estate counsel from an experienced specialist. Statistics show that 68% of home buyers work with the very first real estate agent they meet. And over 85% work with the first or second real estate professional they meet. If you were choosing a doctor to perform a special procedure, would you choose the first one you meet? Probably not without asking the doctor some important questions like – how long have you been doing this procedure? What is your survival rate? Is this your specialty? My advice is to choose your real estate professional wisely.

**SECRET REVEALED: For better or worse, 68% of home buyers work with the first agent they meet – regardless of their experience or qualifications.**

Real estate professionals get paid on average about the same fee, 3%± of the sales price of the home, regardless of experience or training. Even though I have over twenty-five years experience and have helped literally thousands of home buyers through the process, I get paid about the same amount per transaction as the agent who just earned their license and who has very little experience. In other professional industries, the fees usually increase with the professional's experience. Not necessarily so with real estate.

# Hire a Buyer's Broker

Engage a buyer's broker (agent). As a buyer, you have the right to exclusive buyer's representation. The real estate industry is set up a little different than other industries. The inventory of homes for sale is controlled by seller's representatives. All of those signs you see and all of those advertisements are posted by "listing" agents who work for the seller or builder. That's right, all of those nice agents and savvy on-site builders agents don't represent you. They represent the seller. Their job is to get the seller (or builder) the best price and terms. It is their legal, contractual responsibility to get the seller (not you) the best deal. You as a buyer have the right to have your own representation when buying a home. In fact, the fee for your buyer agent's representation is already accounted for and paid for by the agreement with the seller and the seller's agent. In a typical transaction, a seller agrees to pay a 6% commission (although fees are not set by rules or law and vary). Out of a typical 6% commission, 3% would be paid to the listing agent, the one who puts the sign in the yard and is marketing it for sale. And the other 3% is offered to pay any buyer's broker who brings a buyer (you) who purchases the home. So, the fee for your representation has already been agreed to be paid for by the seller. If you don't have your own agent then you throw away your right to representation. If you buy the home directly from the seller's agent (listing agent) the seller's agent keeps the entire 6% ± and you as the buyer get no representation.

**SECRET REVEALED: You have the right to your own representation and the seller/builder pays for it.**

For more information about what to expect in a real estate professional visit: www.RealEstateCoach.Biz.

# Don't Buy Direct

Time and time again, I see home buyers purchase directly from listing agents or builder's on-site representatives without their own agent. They think they can get a better deal going directly to the agent who has the sign in the yard because the seller won't have to pay a buyer's agent – wrong! Listing agents are under no obligation to share their commission with you. And builder's on-site sales agents won't tell a buyer about all the hidden incentives and bonuses the builder is offering. On the other hand, a buyer's agent's job is to get you the best deal. They will negotiate with the seller or builder to get to the very bottom line and at times, below the bottom line. Reputable high volume real estate brokers have more negotiating power than you. When I bring a home buyer to a new home builder neighborhood, I may have already sold a dozen homes this year with that builder. As a high volume agent, I may sell a dozen more with that same builder over the next year. You as a home buyer may only buy one home in a lifetime from this builder. But I may sell millions of dollars of inventory for this builder. Don't you think the builder would be more willing to give my clients a better price to keep my clients and me happy? Builders won't discount the price of a home if you don't have a real estate agent. In most areas of the nation, builders "cooperate" (meaning they pay real estate agent's fees) as part of their marketing expense. Rarely will a builder reduce the price of the home if you don't have an agent. Why? If agents find out that buyers can go direct to a builder and get a better deal directly without an agent, the agents will not continue to support this builder knowing they could possible be cut out. In my area of the country, 70-80% of new homes are sold by real estate agents. If agents find out builders are doing cut rate deals to non-represented home buyers, they could lose 70-80% of their business.

**SECRET REVEALED: Onsite builder representatives won't tell you all the hidden incentives available to you.**

## Respected Agents Have "Influence"

Having a well respected high volume real estate agent on your side can make all the difference in getting you a better deal. Or for that matter even getting the home at all. When I call a listing agent about a home, I will usually get better and more complete information from the listing agent than a buyer would. Brokers have a lingo that can communicate to each other information that is helpful that non-represented home buyers would never be privy to. A buyer calling off a sign or an advertisement are not taken nearly as seriously as a reputable real estate professional with pre-qualified clients in his car. You will actually get treated better by listing agents and builder's on-site agents if you tell them you have a reputable broker on your side. Even if you have not chosen one yet, tell the seller's representative that you will have your own real estate professional involved. Let's say you stop by an "open house" or visit a builder's model home project. Just tell the seller's representative that you will have your own representation. This will show that you will have a knowledgeable and informed expert on your side. Believe it or not, you will be treated with more respect when you say you have your own representation, even if your agent is not with you at the time you visit an open house or a model home.

**SECRET REVEALED: Your agents "reputation" may help you get a better deal.**

## What About For Sale Owners?

Buyer's agents can also be helpful negotiating with "for sale by owner" homes. The owner is usually willing to pay a buyer's agent commission. What the owner is really trying to save is the listing agent's commission. So, if you find a for sale by owner you want to see, tell your agent and they will arrange it.

## Advocacy

Your personal real estate professional is your "advocate." They not only help you find and negotiate a great deal on a home, they will help coordinate the entire process. It's great to have an experienced guide on your side. You will be glad to have an advocate working with you to bounce ideas and questions off of. The real value of a buyer's agent can come when things get rough. When a transaction gets rocky, you need an experienced agent on your side to roll up their sleeves and help fix the problem, or if need be get you out of a purchase and move you on to another home.

An advocate is someone who "is called alongside" to help. Someone who has your best interest in mind. Find and work with advocates and your life will be much easier.

**SECRET REVEALED: Your real estate professional is your "advocate."**

## I Can Help You Be "Referred"

If you need help finding a good real estate professional, let me help. I have relationships with the top real estate professionals all across the nation. If you need help finding a great agent in your town – I will help you.

## Secrets Revealed Recap

1. Get excited, then hire trusted advisors.

2. The real estate broker/agent and lender will coordinate 90% of home buying activities.

3. There are real estate professional who are "experts." Find them and employ them.

4. For better or worse, 68% of home buyers work with the first agent they meet – regardless of their experience or qualifications.

5. You have the right to your own representation and the seller/builder pays for it.

6. Onsite builder representatives won't tell you all the hidden incentives available to you.

7. Your agents "reputation" may help you get a better deal.

8. Your real estate professional is your "advocate."

# Step Four – Apply for Financing

The next step in the home buying process is to apply for a home loan and obtain a pre-approval letter. For many years, I owned and operated a mortgage company so I have insight and knowledge about the loan business. I realized that to address the subject properly, I needed an entire chapter and probably a book to cover all that can be shared on the subject of home mortgages for first timers.

Chapter Seven – "Home Loan Secrets Revealed" is dedicated to additional home loan secrets and you will want to review that chapter prior to applying for a home loan.

## Seek a Trusted Lender Not an Interest Rate

Many first timers will start searching for a home loan or a lender on the internet or in the newspaper. This way of finding a home loan can be hit or miss at best and at worst, a down right disaster. Home buyers start looking for the "best rates" and the "lowest" down payment. This can lead to trouble. What a buyer should be looking for is a "trusted advisor," a loan professional with an excellent track record with the buyer's best interest in mind – not an interest rate! Your real estate professional will know several reputable lenders. A good loan officer can often be found by asking other trusted professionals in related industries. If a friend, relative, or co-worker has had a great experience with a loan officer, you may want to interview their recommendation. Ask your accountant or attorney for a recommendation. Ask them to answer honestly – "who are the 'good ones'." "Who would you send your family member to?" The trusted loan officer is a key member of your team of home buying advisors.

**SECRET REVEALED: Find a loan expert not an interest rate.**

Once you have interviewed a few excellent prospective lenders, you will make an appointment to meet one of them to fill out a loan application. You may be asked to fill out a preliminary application online. The lender may also want to check your credit score ahead of time to save time when you meet. Although you may begin the process online, I recommend that you apply for a home loan in person with your selected lender. A face-to-face meeting will help prevent mistakes that could be made on an online application that could disrupt the process later on.

**SECRET REVEALED: Your lender is a key professional in your home buying process – choose wisely.**

## The Loan Officer and Loan Processor

The lending professionals that you will be involved with are your:

1.    Loan Officer
2.    Loan Processor

**The Loan Officer** is the consultant whom you will make application with. They will analyze your situation and present several lending options. You will discuss down payment, closing costs estimates, interest rates, etc. You will discuss your personal financial status and other factors that may affect your loan. Lending "do's and don'ts" will be discussed. The loan officer is responsible for overseeing the loan process from beginning to end. After your initial application and credit check you will receive a "pre-approval" letter that you may give to your real estate agent to be presented with your purchase offers.

**Loan Processor** – Once you have completed the loan application the Loan Processor gathers and organizes all the documentation for your home loan to be approved. Info is gathered from you and from outside vendors involved in the loan process such as appraisers, credit reporting agencies, title & escrow, etc. During the loan process, you will be speaking with the loan processor and providing items to complete the loan file.

# The Good Faith Estimate

The official name of the form for a loan cost breakdown is the "Good Faith Estimate of Closing Costs." It will show you what interest rate and fees will be charged for your loan and will help you compare with the other lenders you may interview. Not all lenders charge the same interest rates and fees so the good faith will help when comparing.

As of January 2010, lenders are required to use a new standardized good faith estimate of closing costs. This is a form that will show you the up front charges (closing costs) and the prepaid expenses. The new good faith estimate (AKA a G.F.E.) was designed to better inform the borrowers what kind of loan they are applying for and make it easier to compare different loans and lenders' charges. Unfortunately, it has fallen short in a few ways. The new G.F.E. does not tell you what your total payment will be – P.I.T.I. + M.I. Nor does it tell you the total cost of getting a home loan (closing costs, prepaid expenses, and down payment). You will need a separate cost itemization and payment breakdown to get the full picture in detail. The good news is that the new G.F.E. forces lenders to be more accurate as to their true charges. This will help at closing time, as lenders can't surprise you with higher fees and interest rates at the last minute.

**SECRET REVEALED – The "New" Good Faith Estimate will help you compare lender charges.**

# The Application

The standard loan application form that most home lenders use is called F.N.M.A. form 1003. On the application, you will provide your residence and your job history for at least two years. If you already found a home to buy, the address and purchase terms of that home will be provided. You will provide a financial statement including your income, your assets and your debts. There is a short questionnaire regarding residency status and if you have ever filed for bankruptcy/foreclosure, etc.

Your lender will ask you to bring your income and asset documentation. It is a good idea to ask your lender for a list of all items that they will need up front. The more thorough and complete your paperwork up front is, the better. A typical documentation list will include:

1. Two years of W2s and possibly two years of tax returns
2. Most recent paystubs covering one month's wages
3. Two to three months of bank statements and 401k statements
4. Anything else your lender asked you to bring up front

**SECRET REVEALED: The more complete your information is up front the quicker and easier it will be to get a loan approval.**

## The Four Basic Questions You Want Answers To

Most home buyers have four basic questions they want answered when they meet with a lender.

1. Do I qualify for a home loan?
2. How much can I qualify for?
3. How much will my monthly payment be?
4. How much will it cost to buy a home?

## How much do I qualify for?

You will want to know the maximum amount you qualify for. This will be based on your income-to-debt ratios. Although you don't have to buy a home at your maximum qualifying power it is nice to know your limit. Lenders use a percentage of your gross income and your monthly debts to determine your "income to debt ratios." The total home payment plus your other monthly debts will be added together and then divided into your gross monthly income. This will determine your income-to-debt ratio. Most lenders will not allow your income-to-debt ratio to exceed 42% to 50% depending on credit score. Knowing your maximum qualifying home payment will let you know the maximum home price you can shop for.

## How much will my payment be?

Your total payment will be made up of principle, interest, taxes, and insurance (P.I.T.I.). If you are putting less than 20% down, you will most likely pay mortgage insurance (M.I.P. or P.M.I.). Interest rates fluctuate up and down daily. Rate fluctuations are usually small ones but at times can become volatile. However, a quick hike in interest rates will affect your potential payment and your qualifying power. So you will want your lender to keep you informed about rates during your buying process. Property taxes are based on a percentage of the assessed value of the home. This varies from home to home so you will be getting an estimate from your lender until you find a particular property. Homeowner's insurance ranges between $40 to $90 per month depending on coverage and who you choose as your insurance company. M.I.P and P.M.I are based on a percentage of the loan amount and your lender will provide you with the current rates. Your total P.I.T.I. + MI will be around .7% to 1% per month of the loan amount borrowed at the current interest rates at the time this book was written.

## How much will it cost to buy a home?

The cost to purchase a home will include your closing costs, pre-paid expenses, and your down payment (which is really not a cost but becomes part of your "equity"). Closing costs are one-time charges associated with obtaining the home loan. Pre-paid expenses are funds collected up front to establish an escrow account for taxes and insurance and to pay your homeowner's insurance premium for the first year up front (thus "pre-paid"). Your housing costs run about 2-3% of the sales price and your pre-paids are 1-2% of the sales price. The minimum down payment ranges from 0-3.5% of the sales price. Depending on the loan program, your total up front cost is between 3%-8.5% of the sales price. If you can negotiate with the seller to pay some or all of your closing costs, you can cut the cost of getting into a home in half. If you qualify for zero down and have the seller pay closing costs and pre-paids, you can actually buy a home "zero total move-in."

**SECRET REVEALED: You can still purchase a home with as little as 0-3.5% - total move-in.**

# Pre-approval Letter

Once all the preliminary documents are reviewed, you will be issued a letter of pre-approval. A letter of pre-approval is the lender's reasonable assurance that with the information provided and the current credit scores, that you can get a loan. The loan is only "pre-approved" because for a loan to be fully approved, it has to be completely processed. The letter of pre-approval is now almost a required document when making an offer on a home. The seller will want to know that a reputable lender has ran credit and reviewed income and asset documentation. A pre-approval letter can make the difference between a seller taking your offer or some other buyer's offer.

**SECRET REVEALED: A pre-approval letter from a reputable lender can make the difference whether your offer is accepted over another.**

# Some Dos and Don'ts

Dos:

1) Check with your loan officer before making financial moves
2) Keep your cash and reserve levels up

3) Provide your lender with updated financial info such as new pay stubs and bank statements as you get them
4) Carefully document bank balance increases
5) Provide your lender with what they ask for in a timely manner
6) Stay employed

Don'ts:

1) Don't run up balances on credit cards
2) Don't apply for new credit (credit cards, signature loans)
3) Don't buy a car or big consumer items
4) Don't co-sign for new credit with anyone
5) Don't make large bank deposits that are not "paper trailed"
6) Don't pay off old collection accounts
7) Don't close long standing charge accounts
8) Don't switch employment (if possible)

**SECRET REVEALED: Keep in close contact with your lender when making any financial or employment moves.**

# Final Approval

After your loan is processed it is submitted to underwriting for final approval. Loan underwriting is at first done by a computer which will produce a quick answer and produce a list of "conditions." Conditions are clarifications or documentation required by the underwriter to help them make a decision on the home loan. You will receive what is called a conditional approval. You will then provide the loan processor the "conditions" requested. The loan processor will submit conditions to the underwriter who will "sign off" on outstanding conditions. Once all conditions are signed off you will have "full loan approval." At this point, the loan funds are ready and closing can happen quickly when you find a home. If you can start out your home search with a conditional or final loan approval, you will be way ahead of the game. You don't have to wait for final approval to start shopping, but it is nice to have.

**SECRET REVEALED: A fully approved loan is like having a suitcase full of cash ready to purchase any home that meets your parameters.**

Your ability to qualify for a home loan is determined by your – cash, credit, debt, and income. I cover these areas more in detail in Chapter Seven – "Home Loan Secrets Revealed."

If credit scores are an issue, you may have to take steps to repair your credit before going forward in the home buying process. Credit repair is covered in Chapter Six – "Credit Repair Secrets Revealed."

# Secrets Revealed Recap

1. Find a loan expert not an interest rate.

2. Your lender is a key professional in your home buying process – choose wisely.

3. The "New" Good Faith Estimate will help you compare lender charges.

4. The more complete your information is up front the quicker and easier it will be to get a loan approval.

5. You can still purchase a home with as little as 0-3.5% – total move-in.

6. A pre-approval letter from a reputable lender can make the difference whether your offer is accepted over another.

7. Keep in close contact with your lender when making any financial or employment moves.

8. A fully approved loan is like having a suitcase full of cash ready to purchase any home that meets your parameters.

# Step Five – Find Property

## Internet Searches

Statistics show that 90% of homebuyers start their search on the Internet. Today, there is more information available to homebuyers than ever before. Homebuyers now have access to most of the homes on the market through IDX sites that tie into the databases real estate professionals use to market their homes to other real estate professionals. This database is called the Multiple Listing Service or MLS. You have to be a licensed real estate professional and a paying member of the MLS to list properties on the MLS. Today, there are many different portals that can access the homes available on the MLS. For instance, Realtor.com provides MLS listings. This has empowered homebuyers and given them more control over home searches than ever before. In the recent past, the MLS information was accessible only to real estate professionals. Member real estate professionals were able to keep the information exclusive so buyers were forced to contact a real estate professional to find out about homes for sale in any given market. Not so any longer. Having access to home listings has its advantages and disadvantages to buyers. However, the advantages are obvious; at any time, a home buyer can jump on the internet and search homes, get information, view photos and virtual tours, locate them with mapping tools and satellite photos, etc. The emerging generation of homebuyers want more freedom and access to home listings without having to always go through a "middle man." Home buyers want information "now" and the internet provides that instant access. Buyers can set up custom searches and have listings emailed to them whenever a home comes on the market.

**SECRET REVEALED: Information about homes on the internet is incomplete.**

The access to information is helpful, but potentially misleading. Here's why:

1) Most, but not all, of the homes available on the market are not listed in the MLS. For example, many home builders do not put all of their inventory in the MLS. So a buyer might miss the perfect home offered by a homebuilder because it was not listed.

2) Another disadvantage of buyers accessing MLS listings is that the seller's representatives submit the listings. The seller's agent has a responsibility to get the seller the most money and the best terms. Furthermore, if a buyer purchases a home directly from the seller's agent, the fee that the seller has already agreed to pay for the buyer's representation is kept by the listing agent. Also, if there is a better home down the street that is a better fit, the listing agent would not be obligated to tell the buyer.

3) It is the important information that is not listed in the listing data that can lead to un-informed decisions. For instance, the "sold" data is not listed on consumer based IDX Internet sites. The "sold" data is important because that is how real estate professionals determine a home's value. An analysis of sold data will show if sales prices have gone up or down for a neighborhood. Don't rely on internet sites like Zillow or Trulia for market value. Although helpful, these sites rely heavily on tax assessment data for computing a home's value. This tax value provided by the county can be off by tens of thousands of dollars compared to "real" market value. Information that is common knowledge to real estate professionals about home values are not be readily available on internet sites or "MLS listings." Nor will they include information affecting an area such as special assessments or the odorous landfill just over the hill.

**SECRET REVEALED: "Sold" data is not readily available on the internet.**

Doing your own research and studying the areas and trends on the internet is helpful and can save time, but you are advised to engage the services of a knowledgeable, full-time professional who represents you to fill in the gaps of knowledge and continue to guide you to the property that will be "right" for you.

**SECRET REVEALED: The internet can be a good source of information but not a good source of wisdom.**

## New Vs. Resale

I often get asked the question – "which is better, to buy a new home or a resale home?" and my answer is always "that depends." There are advantages and disadvantages to both. First, new homes tend to be "further out." As the city grows, the builders move further out to build on land at the fringe of the city. In large metropolitan areas there are new "in fill" projects where builders will tear down older homes and build new ones. This can get you "closer in" but you may be surrounded by an older neighborhood.

## New Homes

New homes are attractive because they are "new." Never lived in. The appliances are new, the structure is new, there will be no need to worry about fixing things, painting, or re-carpeting. New homes come with warranties provided by the builder. Usually the home is warranted "bumper to bumper" for the first one to two years, and the major structural components are usually warranted for ten years. If you decide to build a home from the ground up, you will be involved with how the house comes together along with the help of a builder's decorator. You will be able to choose cabinets, carpet, tile, counters, color schemes, etc. and upgrades that go into the home.

**SECRET REVEALED: New homes are warranted for one to ten years.**

If you build a home with a national builder, you will go to a decorating center where you can view the many selections and upgrade options that can be put into your new home. A decorator will assist you in "putting it all together." One thing to be careful of is to not go overboard with decorating. Some of the highest builder profit margins are in the "upgrades." There is a builder markup in every upgrade choice. In a first home, it is important to not "over build" for the neighborhood. Your real estate professionals can be a great resource for helping you determine what is necessary to put into the home and which upgrades will be helpful in reselling the home later on. They'll know what is common for the neighborhood and what is not. If all the homes have three side masonry and one side paneling, it will be a luxury to upgrade to a fourth side masonry house.

**SECRET REVEALED: Don't go overboard at the decorating center.**

Although new homes are attractive for their "newness." New home subdivisions tend to be "further out." Also, during the construction period, it can be hard to "picture" a neighborhood. New home neighborhoods are young so the landscaping and foliage may take some time to mature. I personally enjoy selling brand new homes to my clients. For secrets to getting the best deal from a builder refer to Chapter Eight – "Home Builder Secrets Revealed."

# Resale Homes

Resale homes have the advantage of being "broken in." Homes that have been lived in have a lot of the kinks worked out. The owners have spent money fixing up the home, adding improvements, landscaping, etc. Another advantage of resale homes is the fact that they are existing – no need to make building decisions. You can also see the neighborhood and the neighboring homes. The foliage and landscaping is already established. Resale homes tend to be "closer in" because of the nature of urban & suburban sprawl. In most markets, you will have a selection of new and resale to choose from. Have your real estate professional discuss with you the pros and cons of new and resale in your area.

**SECRET REVEALED: Resale homes are "broken in" and have more mature foliage.**

# Up Front Monies

Once you have found a home, you will be asked to provide funds for a number of "up front" expenses. The first is earnest money. Earnest money are funds that are paid into a title or escrow company that show the seller of the home you are "serious." It usually amounts to ½ of 1% or more of the offered price. This money is set aside and becomes part of your funds to close. Earnest money is at risk if you back out of the purchase contract for no good reason. However, you will have a chance to have the property inspected for problems or deficiencies and you will pay a small fee called an "option fee" which gives you the "unrestricted right to terminate" during the first week or two of the contract period. This is usually $100-$250 and is usually applied to closing. If you don't like what you find in the inspection or just change your mind, the small option fee will be forfeited and you can cancel, get your earnest money back and move on to another home.

**SECRET REVEALED: Earnest money shows the seller you are serious.**

# Inspection Money

When you find a home and enter into a purchase agreement, you will have the property inspected by a state licensed inspector. This fee runs between $250 & $400. There may also be a termite inspection which is usually $75 to $100.

Further inspections could be ordered, such as a foundation inspection, but property & termite are the common ones.

## Appraisal & Credit Report Fees

Your lender may require you to pay for an appraisal and credit report up front to pay for these services. Some lenders will "front" these fees to you and collect them at closing.

So in review, your up front monies that you need to be prepared for before entering into a contract are:

1. Earnest Money – ½ to 1% (or more) of sales price
2. Option Fee – $100 to $250 (not required in some states)
3. Inspection Fee – $250 to $400
4. Termite Inspection – $75 to $100
5. Appraisal & Credit Report – $300

**SECRET REVEALED: Be prepared for some up front expenses before you buy a home.**

## Your Home Tour

You will need to set aside two to four hours for a home tour. Real estate professionals are accustomed to scheduling tours around work schedules, or on evenings and weekends. Ideally, you may want to schedule a day off from work to tour homes. Days off are great for touring because you will be more relaxed and focused.

Your real estate professional will line up usually between five and ten homes that fit your criteria. Finding the right home is a process of elimination and the quicker you eliminate homes, the closer you will be to finding "the right one." I tell my clients – if you don't really like the neighborhood or the home from the outside as you drive up, then don't waste time going through a home. Your time is better spent heading to the next one.

Although, in a few rare cases I have had buyers purchase a home they first thought was ugly from the outside but this is the rare exception. If the neighborhood or the home's appearance repulses you – move on! I find it helpful for home buyers to drive around ahead of time to some of the target neighborhoods and drive by some of the chosen listings. This can help save time and eliminate homes and areas that don't work.

**SECRET REVEALED: Do "drive bys" to help eliminate homes and areas.**

# Electronic Key Access

Another great thing about having your trusted real estate professional escorting you around is that they have electronic access to all of the homes listed. Real estate professionals have an electronic key that allows them access to almost any property listed by any other real estate broker. They will also call the owner ahead of time to let them know you are coming. This way the occupant can vacate ahead of time and take their prized yippee poodle or video game-playing teenagers with them so you can view the home without distractions. Having electronic access saves you time and is much more convenient.

**SECRET REVEALED: Electronic home access is much more convenient and time saving.**

# The Grading System

It is very helpful to use a grading system when you tour homes. Use an A, B, C, D, or scale of 1-to-10 (with 10 being perfect) when touring homes. Grade the neighborhood, the location, the condition, the floor plan, the functionality and special features, but really the overall rating for the home is what will be the most important. The reason being is you may see many homes in a day and grading will help separate the "wannabes" from the real candidates. Usually a few rise to the top and those are the ones that you will want to re-visit on your next tour. If you find one that really fits the bill – 9.5s or perfect 10s – then don't hesitate to let your real estate professional know. You may want to get serious about buying it now before it sells to someone else. Remember that there are other buyers looking at the same homes and the good ones sell first. It is tough on you and your real estate agent to have to compare all the rest of the homes to "the one you missed." In a seller's market, you will have to make quicker decisions and make offers right away or you may miss out on home after home. In a buyer's market, you will have more time to make thorough decisions, but even in a buyer's market – the good ones go first.

**SECRET REVEALED: Even in a buyer's market, the good homes sell first.**

# The Neighborhood

Neighborhoods vary from area to area. Even from street to street. It is a good idea to check out school districts, crime ratings, traffic patterns, as well as future potential impacts to a community. Your real estate professional will most likely know some of these "stats" but it will be up to you to research the area. If you question the neighborhood's character, knock on a few doors and talk with a few of the residents. If you are more than curious, you may want to come back and check it out on a Saturday night and see who's "hanging out." The saying goes "you can't choose your neighbors" so you may want to respectfully check out the neighbors as part of your due diligence. An important consideration is traffic patterns and traffic noise. I remember one of the first homes I purchased. After I bought it I noticed that the street had a double yellow line down the middle of the road. Since my home was the first home to be built on the street, it didn't alarm me, but as the neighborhood grew, I realized that this street was a thoroughfare and it became very busy. Later on, it was one of my primary motivations for me to move, especially when I considered the safety of my small children.

**SECRET REVEALED: Be aware – you can't choose your neighbors or change traffic patterns.**

# Schools

Schools and school districts are important considerations. Even if you are single or not planning a family – consider the schools. The quality of schools can have a direct impact on home values and future sale ability of the home. You can find school ratings on the state department of education websites.

When you get serious about an area, make an appointment to visit the school of choice and take a tour. Administrators are happy to show parents around and discuss their educational programs. Schools are important, so take their quality seriously.

**SECRET REVEALED: Schools and school districts have a direct impact on value and desirability.**

# Secrets Revealed Recap

1. Information about homes on the internet is incomplete at best.

2. "Sold" data is not readily available on the internet.

3. The internet can be a good source of information but not a good source of wisdom.

4. New homes are warranted for one to ten years.

5. Don't go overboard at the decorating center.

6. Resale homes are "broken in" and have more mature foliage.

7. Earnest money shows the seller you are serious.

8. Be prepared for some up front expenses before you buy a home.

9. Do "drive bys" to help eliminate homes and areas.

10. Electronic home access is much more convenient and time saving.

11. Even in a buyer's market, the good homes sell first.

12. Be aware – you can't choose your neighbors or change traffic patterns.

13. Schools and school districts have a direct impact on value and desirability.

# Step Six – Negotiate Agreement

# Initial Contact with Listing Agent

Once you get serious about making an offer on a home, your real estate professional will contact the listing (seller's) agent and ask questions about the seller's "situation." This call is 1to probe the listing agent to get clues as to the urgency and motivation of the seller. Your professional will ask questions like, "When do the sellers want to move?" "How long has the home been on the market?" "Is there anything special we need to know about the home?" "Are there any issues with the property or with the seller?" Your professional will want to know if there are any other offers coming in on the home or if there have been any offers recently. The purpose of these questions is to help structure an offer that will work in your best interest. If the home has been sitting on the market vacant with no offers on it, you will have a better chance at getting a reduced price than if the home has multiple offers on it. Technically, the listing (seller's) agent should not disclose any information about price and terms other than what is listed (unless the seller authorizes it) but at times listing agents disclose information that will be in the buyer's favor when negotiating. Remember, your real estate professional's job is to use whatever information or knowledge they have to get you a better deal. If the listing agent discloses helpful info in your favor, great!

Another reason for having your professional make the call is that they will get better and more complete information than if you called the listing agent directly. A listing agent takes another agent's call much more seriously than a "sign" call.

Another phenomenon I have experienced is the unwritten language that professionals use. The lingo we use in agent to agent conversation will reveal possible clues that will help you get a better deal. Terms like "motivated" "flexible" "firm" or "tough" give us clues to the seller's situation.

**SECRET REVEALED: Buyer's Agents will get better and more complete information than a buyer would.**

# The Offer

Your goal is to negotiate the best deal for you. Keep in mind that the best deal should be a win-win for all involved. Your real estate professional will sit down with you and prepare an offer to purchase. This purchase contract or purchase agreement will spell out all the terms and conditions that will have to be satisfied in order for you to buy the home. Your offer is just that – an offer. Your real estate professional will go over the purchase agreement point by point, paragraph by paragraph. For resale (used) homes, the state provides real estate agents with standardized agreements with blanks to be completed. Builders often have their own purchase agreements which their management and attorneys have approved of.

If you have any legal or tax questions or concerns, it is best to consult with your attorney and/or CPA when making an offer.

**SECRET REVEALED: Real estate professionals are not qualified to give tax or legal advice. Seek proper counsel.**

You and your real estate professional will discuss the terms and timing for the offer including but not limited to – price, down payment, type of financing, place of closing, who will pay closing costs, inspection periods, and more. The purchase agreement in our state is a minimum of fourteen pages long. It is important that you have "your" hired real estate professional fill out this agreement (and not the seller's agent) as there are ramifications on each page and paragraph of the purchase agreement. You will most likely offer a lower price than what the seller is asking (list price). However, if the home is priced well to begin with – full price may be the "best price." And in a seller's market or in a multiple offer situation "more than full price" can at times be advisable. Remember, great homes priced well are often the first to sell. So even in a buyer's market, great, well-priced properties can go for more than full price.

**SECRET REVEALED: Sometimes full price is the best price.**

# The Art of Negotiation

Negotiating the best price and terms for a home is an art. And like most art forms, it requires practice and expertise. It's another reason why you want your real estate agent to be an excellent negotiator (I recommend making this a top requirement in your choice of professionals). You and your agent will write the offer. Your agent will then present the offer to the listing agent along with the loan pre-approval letter and a copy of the earnest money and option checks. A nice touch is when the buyer writes a pleasant note to the seller about how they would like to make this their home. The listing agent will then present the offer to the owners. In almost all cases – you as a buyer do not negotiate directly with the seller. In fact, I find it wise to not have the buyer and seller meet each other. The reason being is that personalities can get in the way of good business and can be counter productive to all involved.

**SECRET REVEALED: Make sure your agent is a negotiation "artist."**

The listing agent and seller will either accept the offer as written, "counter," or reject. A counter offer is normal. The sellers will make changes that work better for them. Then the offer will be sent back to your agent for review and for your approval or counter offer. This process can go back and forth several times until all points of the contract are agreed upon. Once all points are agreed to, the contract will be "executed" and the process to "close" begins. Once the contract is executed, the earnest money is deposited at a third party escrow/title company along with the contract.

# Agent's Reputation

Believe it or not, your agent's reputation and track record will also make a difference in both the quantity and quality of information you can get from a listing agent and how seriously they take your offer. A highly reputable, high volume real estate professional making the call to the listing agent will carry more weight than a "weekend warrior" part-time agent. They know the "heavy hitter" real estate professionals are much more likely to have a "serious & motivated" buyer and will more likely get the deal done. Recently, I was able to get my client's offer accepted over another identical offer written by another agent because the listing agent knew me and my track record of getting homes closed. Furthermore, if you have a real estate agent that is difficult to deal with, it can actually hurt your chances of getting the home. Once again, this is another reason for you to hire the best representation you can find.

**SECRET REVEALED: Your agent's "reputation" can help you or hurt you.**

# Watch Out For Buyer's Remorse

Buyer's remorse is a common phenomenon that happens in nearly every home purchase. It is important that you work through it. Let's face it, buying a home is a big commitment. Buying a home ranks in the top five most stressful things you can do. So, emotions run high and pressure can build and sometimes you get confused or just freeze and don't want to move. During the process, you will feel buyer's remorse. Take heart, every home I purchased I have felt a tinge or a full blown case of buyer's remorse but then I come to my senses and continue on with the process. The important thing to know is that it is common and in the end, it will all work out. I let my clients know when they sign a contract that they will have buyer's remorse. I encourage them to call me to work through it. When dealing with couples, I let them both know that it is a possibility and that they should encourage each other. My hope is that they both don't have it at the same time. The common times for "remorse" are at contract and when you get close to closing. Work through it and know that it is normal.

**SECRET REVEALED: Watch out for buyer's remorse – it can cost you your home.**

# Secrets Revealed Recap

1. Buyer's Agents will get better and more complete information than a buyer would.

2. Real estate professionals are not qualified to give tax or legal advice. Seek proper counsel.

3. Sometimes full price is the best price.

4. Make sure your agent is a negotiation "artist."

5. Your agent's "reputation" can help you or hurt you.

6. Watch out for "buyer's remorse" – it can cost you your home.

## Step Seven – Contract Processed

Once your purchase agreement has been executed and your earnest money deposited with the escrow/title company, the process towards closing (home ownership) begins. A flurry of activity takes place once your contract is executed. The escrow/title company cashes your earnest money and puts it in their account for safe keeping to be applied toward your down payment and closing costs. Your "option" period begins. This is the period of time that you will have to complete your inspections and get estimates for any repairs that may need to be done. The option period is usually from one to two weeks. In some states there is an automatic option period set by statute. In our state (Texas) the option period is negotiable. You may be required to pay the seller a small fee to give you the "option" to back out during the option period. If you decide to back out during the option period, you will lose your small option fee but your earnest money will be refunded to you. In our state, this option period gives a buyer the "unrestricted right" to back out for any reason. The most common reason to back out is that the property doesn't pass the inspection. This is also your "buyer's remorse" period. I tell my clients, "If you don't like which way the wind blows on this home, you can back out during the option period."

**SECRET REVEALED: Your option period gives you the right to back out at little or no cost.**

## Home Loan is Updated & Processed

Along with your option period, you will have a financing contingency period. Although you are already pre-approved with a lender, you will now move toward full loan approval. Your purchase contract will be forwarded to your lender and an appraisal of the property will be ordered. Not only do you have to be approved for the loan but the property does too. The appraisal is performed by a state licensed appraiser who will determine the fair market value of the home. The appraiser will also note any items that need to be repaired in accordance with the lending institutions' guidelines.

Over the next few days, your lender will ask for updated financial information such as pay stubs and bank statements and the credit report will be updated. Updated employment verification and rental history will be ordered. A title policy and the seller's loan pay off amount will be ordered. The financial documents appraisal, credit report, and title work will be packaged up and then be sent to an underwriter for full loan approval.

# Conditions Satisfied

The fourteen page (+) agreement you signed is filled with conditions that need to be satisfied before you can close. Every paragraph in the agreement contains conditions or "contingencies" that will be satisfied as you work through the process. The good news is most of these conditions are handled by the professionals that are employed to make your transaction happen. Your job is to cooperate as much as possible with the requests from your lender and your real estate professional. The flurry of activities begins to increase again as you near closing.

**Secret Revealed: Cooperate with requests from your real estate professional and lender.**

The underwriter may need written clarification or explanations regarding your loan file. Provide your lender with everything they request in a timely manner. Although you may have already given the information or explanations – give it to them again if requested. Whatever you do, do not apply for credit, buy items on credit like refrigerators, appliances, bedroom suites, as these purchases and inquiries can show up last minute on your credit report. Whatever you do, do not buy a new car on credit.

I remember the case where a buyer was purchasing a home with a Veterans Administration loan and signed his final V.A. "disclosure forms." He thought it was the final closing documents but the closing was not until the following week. He then went out and bought a Corvette. The lender found out about it when they ran a final credit report – the new car payments disqualified him from getting the home. Ooops, he had a new Corvette and no garage to park it in. Buying the car blew his financing.

**SECRET REVEALED: Buy the house before you buy the car.**

Fortunately, he had a relative pay off the car for him but it was embarrassing and he was almost "homeless." Funny thing is, he would have been able to go and finance a new car the day after he closed on the home – but not the other way around.

As we near closing, lending and title company conditions are satisfied. Agreements you have made with the seller are completed. Review appraisals are completed. Agreed upon home repairs are finished up.

Your real estate professional will coordinate activities with the lender, title company, inspector, and listing agent. Access will be arranged for your inspectors, appraisers, and/or contractors, etc., and utilities will be turned on.

A typical resale home purchase from contract to close is thirty to sixty days. Most of the activities are at the beginning and end of the process. There are dozens of duties performed on your behalf to complete the transaction. Dozens of hard working professionals will be collaborating to get you into your home.

## Secrets Revealed Recap

1. Your option period gives you the right to back out at little or no cost.

2. Cooperate with requests from your real estate professional and lender.

3. Buy the house before you buy the car.

# Step Eight – Home Inspected

## Inspections and Repairs – Resale Homes

As part of the purchase agreement the seller will give you a written seller's disclosure statement. This tells you everything the seller knows that is wrong with the property and any events that have happened that the seller was aware of such as leaks, fires, or insurance claims. But you aren't going to take the seller's word for the condition of the property so you will hire an expert.

**SECRET REVEALED: Don't buy a home without having it inspected.**

## A Licensed Property Inspector

You are encouraged to hire a state licensed property inspector. Your inspector will check out the entire property from top to bottom. Structural items will be inspected such as foundations, roof coverings, walls, doors, windows, fireplaces, even sidewalks and patios.

Electrical systems will be tested, heating and air conditioning systems will be checked to see if there is proper heating and cooling. The attic insulation and duct work will be checked. The plumbing system will be tested to make sure there are no leaks and adequate pressure and temperatures.

All the appliances will be inspected, including the stove, microwave, garbage disposal, etc. Sprinkler systems, swimming pools, septic systems, smoke alarms, even the doorbell is checked to see if it is functioning properly.

The inspections are very thorough and can take several hours to complete. I recommend that you accompany the inspector during the inspection. You will learn a lot about your home and how it functions. You will also learn valuable maintenance tips to keep things running smoothly. I have personally attended hundreds of inspections and I can honestly say I learn something new every time.

**SECRET REVEALED: Try to attend the inspection. You will learn a lot about your home.**

I tell my clients to expect at least three to thirty items to be noted as "needing repair" on an inspection report. This may seem like a lot but it is common. Usually the items needing repair are minor and can be fixed at minimal costs. However, sometimes the findings can be less than favorable like cracked foundations or a roof needing replacement. If there are major items uncovered by the inspector such as a cracked foundation, he will recommend you contact a structural engineer to give repair recommendations.

The inspector will provide you with a written report and summary of the findings and conclusions. You will now want to discuss the report with your inspector and your real estate agent. You may need to get bids from contractors to determine the expense of repair items. Your real estate professional will then make a written request of items to be repaired. The sellers will let you know what they will fix or won't fix or may offer you money and let you hire your own workers to fix the issues. If you cannot come to an agreement on repairs or repair allowances then you will have the option to cancel the purchase and get your earnest money back and move on to another home. Usually there is a compromise, but if not, you can back out and get your earnest money returned. Just make sure you come to agreement during the "option period" or you may lose the right to ask for repairs and if you back out, the seller may try to keep your earnest money.

**SECRET REVEALED: In an inspection report, three to thirty items "needing repair" is common.**

# Pest Inspections

Most homebuyers will opt for a termite inspection. If termites are found, you will be glad you had the inspection because the little bugs can cause a lot of expensive damage. New homes usually do not need to be inspected for termites

Inspections are an important part of the buying process and will give you some piece of mind that your home is safe and sound. I do not recommend purchasing a home without an inspection – especially for a first time homebuyer!

# Final Walk Through

As you are nearing closing day, you will want to do a final walkthrough. The purpose of the final walk is to make sure the repairs that were requested were completed. Make sure the home is in the same condition as when you made your buying decision and that there are no "missing" items that should have remained with the home. You will want to also check that nothing major happened to the home prior to your signing off on it – no floods, fires, or weather damage. You should do your final *final* walkthrough the day of or the day before closing.

# Preparing for Closing

# Utilities

Make sure you call the utility companies several days prior to closing. You don't want to get to your new home the day of closing and find the lights out or no hot water. Utility companies sometimes need deposits or credit checks before opening an account. If you transfer service before they disconnect the utilities, it may prevent the inconvenience of having to wait on them to turn on service.

# Moving Companies & Deliveries

I recommend that you do not schedule movers the same day as closing. It's not fun having a delay at closing and then have movers waiting at the house ready to unload. If possible, schedule the move a day or two after the scheduled closing date. This will save a lot of aggravation in case of a delay at the closing table. The same goes for appliance and new furniture deliveries. Try not to have them delivered the same day as closing. If they have to come back, they may charge you additional fees to re-deliver.

**SECRET REVEALED: Try not to schedule a move on the same day of closing.**

# Young Kids & Pets

Children can sometimes be overwhelmed with the transition from home to home. I suggest having them come to the new home before and maybe during a walk through. Have them pick out their rooms. Let them play in the back yard so they can "picture" themselves in the new surroundings. Pets can have a tough time moving with all the new sights and smells. Take care to keep them safe and secure during the transition. There has been more than one case of a pet "taking off" never to be seen again. So if possible, keep the pets well supervised and nurtured during the move so as to not traumatize them in the transition.

## Secrets Revealed Recap

1.  Don't buy a home without having it inspected.

2.  Try to attend the inspection. You will learn a lot about your home.

3.  In an inspection report, three to thirty items "needing repair" is common.

4.  Try not to schedule a move on the same day of closing.

# Step Nine – Closing

It's the day you've been waiting for. The closing is where you become a homeowner. This is where all the documents and funds will come together. The closing is usually held at a title company, escrow company, or an attorney's office. You will bring your certified funds (cashiers check), your ID, and be ready to sign what seems like an endless stack of documents. All of the documents that you sign and acknowledge will fulfill a specific purpose. Like a big jigsaw puzzle, all the pieces come together at the closing. You'll sign a promissory note, promising to pay back the mortgage. The sellers will deed you the property. You will hand over your share of the funds and the seller will give you the keys to your new home!

## At the Closing

Your real estate professional should be present to answer questions. I suggest having the loan officer at closing too if possible. Surprises can happen at the closing. The best thing you can do is come prepared, stay calm, enjoy the process, and get excited about the fact that you are going to walk away a homeowner.

## Closing Day – Preparing For Close

Your purchase contract will have a specific date for your closing to occur. The purchase agreement may state "on or before" which means that if you and the seller agree and the paperwork is ready, you may choose to close sooner than the date in the purchase agreement. If there are delays for whatever reason, you may extend the contract to a later date if you and the seller agree.

The title or escrow officer or closing attorney is sometimes referred to as a "closer." The closer will also contact you regarding the time for your appointment, remind you of any special requirements, ask you to bring your ID (two forms) and tell you the amount of the funds you will need to bring in. Make sure that the funds you bring to the close are "certified funds" such as a cashier's check. The escrow/title company will not take a personal check for closing (other than small amounts in case there was a last minute adjustment, so bring your checkbook also). You may opt to arrange to wire your funds to the title company, but make sure it is done ahead of time as wires sometimes take a while to clear between banks and can hold up closing.

**SECRET REVEALED: Bring to closing your ID, cashier's check, checkbook, and your spouse.**

If possible, try not to close on the very last day of the month. Escrow and title companies are extremely busy at the end of the month. Closings at the very end of the month can be hurried and more intense.

Closing day can be hectic, so to reduce stress – get your cashier's check the day before and make sure you know where the title company is located. They often have several locations and more than once I have had clients show up to the wrong office location only to have to run across town to the correct office.

**SECRET REVEALED: Try not to close on the last day of the month.**

Whatever you do, make sure you do not open any credit accounts such as store cards or worse buy a car, until <u>after</u> closing. I have experienced occasions where a home buyer purchased a refrigerator or a washer and dryer on credit just before closing and it almost cost them the home because the lender found out about the new debt. Don't fall for the "zero payments, zero interest for two years" offer at the appliance store – it can and show up on credit right when you are trying to close on the house. Applying for credit can be a big oops.

**SECRET REVEALED: Do not apply for new credit until after closing.**

# At Closing

The sellers usually have less paperwork to sign than buyers so they may sign ahead of time or afterward so they don't have to wait around for the buyer to make it through their "stack" of documents. Sometimes sellers and buyers close together at the same time and at the same table. I think it is nice to have the buyers & sellers at least greet each other. It was their home – now it's your home. The sellers may even tell you some humorous or intriguing stories about the home. Of course, if the sellers were under a stressful situation like divorce or financial difficulty, I suggest you close separately.

# The "Stack"

When you get to closing, you will be signing your name more than fifty times. Many of these documents are "boiler plate" disclosure forms. However, some of them can have a dramatic effect on your financial future.

As I mentioned before, you want your real estate professionals present – especially your real estate agent and loan officer, if possible, to help you through the procedure. Your escrow/title officer (closer) will also help you with brief explanations of the documents that you are signing. The brief descriptions given by the closer are helpful but if you have transaction issues or discrepancies in dollar figures, the closer will defer to your representatives and the written contract for answers. Legal questions should be posed to your attorney who should be available at least by phone if need be. The title/ escrow officer is technically a neutral third party, meaning they take no "sides" on decisions agreed upon between the parties to the transaction. The closer's job is also to account for all the dollars & documents changing hands.

One thing to keep in mind – don't try to plan on reading all your documents at closing. It would take several hours for you to read every document and closers don't have the time to sit through your reading. You certainly have the right to read all documents, but it would be best if you have your closer get you the documents a day or two before closing so you can read through them. Otherwise, the closer will most likely put you in another room while you read through them (for hours) and when you are done, they will proceed with your closing.

**SECRET REVEALED: If you want to read all the documents, get them a few days ahead of time to review.**

Documents vary from state to state so check with your real estate professionals for advice. Keep in mind – if you need legal or tax advice about your documents, consult a lawyer or CPA. Documents you will want to review carefully (among others) are the closing statement and the promissory note.

## The Closing Statement

The H.U.D. 1 "settlement statement" – or "closing statement" is commonly the first document that will be reviewed (and one of the most important). The H.U.D. 1 is where the transaction numbers between you, the seller, the mortgage company, title company, and most everyone else involved in your purchase are accounted for. The H.U.D. 1 accounting can be a difficult job for the closer because of all the entities involved and the potential for last minute changes, last minute negotiations, possible errors, and changes in fees, costs and tax prorations. I have attended thousands of closings and more often than not, there will be a change made on the closing statement at the closing table. Usually, I see minor adjustments. In some rare cases, I have seen huge corrections – thousands of dollars – in favor of one party or another. Quality time will be spent going over the settlement statement because that's where the money is accounted for.

**SECRET REVEALED: There are almost always minor (and sometimes major) adjustments to the closing statement.**

# Page One of the Settlement Statement

Page one of the settlement statement details the final math and prorations for purchase transaction. Make sure all the information at the top of the statement is accurate. Name, address, date, etc.

The bottom half of page one is the summary of the transaction for both the buyer and the seller. The left side is the buyer's details and the right side is the seller's. Debits and credits are accounted for between the parties. Section 100 details the total amount due from the buyer, starting with the contract price – make sure it is accurate. The buyer's settlement charges or "closing costs" are brought from the bottom line of page two. Section 200 accounts for credits to the buyer including the earnest money deposit and any additional deposits. The loan amount is credited on line 202. Double-check your figures. Sometimes a deposit figure can be miscalculated or a loan amount could be wrong. Additional prorations and adjustments are made at the bottom of section 200. In section 300, the final math is calculated and your cash to close is located on the "bottom line." This is the amount that you will need to have certified funds for (cashier's check, bank wire, etc). Remember to bring your checkbook for any minor shortages. If there are any credits due back to you, the title company will usually cut you a check on the spot.

# Page Two of the Closing Statement

Sometimes, the closer will start the closing statement review on page two of the closing statement because that is where the settlement charges are accounted for. On page two of the H.U.D. 1 are several sections from the 700s to 1400s. The first section – the 700s – details the commission charges that are usually paid by the seller. The 800s are items payable in connection with the loan.

The 900s account for prorated prepaid interest mortgage insurance and homeowner's or hazard insurance. Your hazard insurance is paid in advance for a full year. Your interest is calculated from the day of closing to the end of the month. Interest on home mortgages is collected in arrears meaning the payments you make on the first of each month pays the interest for the previous month so a pleasant surprise for you is that you will not make a payment the first month you are in the home. So if you close in May, your first home payment will be due in July.

**SECRET REVEALED: You will skip your first month's payment.**

Section 1000s is the breakdown of your reserves and establishment of an escrow account. Your escrow account with your new mortgage company is set up so that each month a part of your payment is set aside to pay your annual taxes & insurance when they are due. With minimum down payments loans, the lender almost always requires an escrow account to be established so the taxes and insurance will be paid. If a buyer puts 20% down then the requirement for an escrow account can be waived and the buyer can pay taxes and insurance when they are due each year rather than having the lender handling it.

The 1100s are title and escrow company charges. This section usually covers the document preparation fees by the attorneys and title insurance to insure good and equitable title to you. You may see courier fees or fed ex charges in this section as well.

The 1200s detail government recording fees and transfer charges. Make sure you give your closing statement to your accountant at tax time because there are potentially thousands in tax deductions. For instance, interest and discount points are deductible – even if paid by the seller.

The 1300s cover remaining fees that were charged in conjunction with the sale including survey, pest inspection, contractors, homeowner's association transfer fees and dues. It is the "bottom line." It details all the buyer's costs and the seller's costs in a lump sum at the bottom of the page.

As of January 2010, RESPA (Real Estate Settlement Producers Act) required all lenders and title companies to adopt a new standardized H.U.D. 1 closing statement. The new closing statement is designed to keep lenders more accountable to their original good faith estimate. Although this is probably a great idea, the way it was designed shows less detail than the previous closing statements. For example, all the loan fees are lumped together as one big fee. Detail-oriented people who want a breakdown and accounting of their loan fees will need to refer to the original good faith estimate and an itemized breakdown of the closing costs.

# Page Three of H.U.D. 1

One feature that has been included in the new closing statement is the 10% rule. The 10% rule requires the total loan origination charges to be within 10% of the original good faith estimate provided by the lender. If it is off by more than 10%, the lender must correct it to get it "in line" with the good faith estimate or "re-disclose" and the closing will have to be pushed back three days. The interest rate must also be within 1/8 of a percent of the last interest rate disclosed by the lender in writing prior to closing. If it is off more than 1/8 of a percent, the closing will have to be postponed for re-disclosure. Although the intentions of these new changes are good, the legally required delays could disrupt those needing to close on a certain day.

Another new feature of the revised H.U.D. 1 statements is the recap of the "loan terms." The recap will cover:

1.  The initial loan amount
2.  Your loan term (how many years)
3.  Your initial interest rate
4.  A breakdown of your initial monthly loan payments
5.  Whether your interest rate is adjustable and how it can adjust
6.  Whether your loan balance could go up (negative amortization)
7.  Whether your loan payment can change
8.  Whether your loan has a penalty for early pay off
9.  Whether your loan has a balloon payment (meaning a large lump sum) due in so many years
10. A breakdown of your total monthly payment

**SECRET REVEALED: There are many tax-deductible items on your closing statement including taxes and interest.**

# Promissory "Note"

You will also want to look closely at your "note." This document is your promise to repay the loan. It will spell out the terms of the loan, the interest rate, and any adjustable features or prepayment penalties. You want to make sure the note matches what was promised to you by your mortgage company.

# Secrets Revealed Recap

1. Bring to closing your ID, cashier's check, checkbook, and your spouse.

2. Try not to close on the last day of the month.

3. Do not apply for new credit until after closing.

4. If you want to read all the documents, get them a few days ahead of time to review.

5. There are almost always minor (and sometimes major) adjustments to the closing statement.

6. You will skip your first month's payment

7. There are many tax-deductible items on your closing statement including taxes and interest.

# Step Ten – Home Ownership

Now that you are a homeowner, you will enjoy the benefits and responsibilities of owning your own share of the American Dream. It's a great feeling to know that you are an owner and are building your equity & net worth by paying down a mortgage. Make sure you put all the paperwork you received from the title company in a safe place. Take time to fill out warranty cards for new appliances. Remember to put your home warranty info in an easily accessible, safe place should you need it.

# Change of Address

Fill out your change of address cards for the post office and let everyone know your new mailing address. All your friends, family, banks, credit cards, magazines, etc. If you need keys to your mailbox, you can go to the post office and show them your closing statement and they will give you keys. Make sure they change the lock out so no one except you can get to your mail. Make sure you change the locks at your new home. You don't know who has copies of the old key so it is important you get the locks changed ASAP. If your home has a security system, make sure to change the password. Get the current code from the former owner and then change it. It is a good idea to get the phone number and forwarding address of the former owners so that if you have questions about the home, you can get in touch with them. You may get mail or packages that are intended for the former owners. They will appreciate you letting them know.

**SECRET REVEALED: Change your locks & security alarm codes after closing.**

If the former owners didn't clean the carpet you probably want to have that done. This is another reason not to try to move in the same day of closing. This is a great time to have new flooring put in if you had that in mind. Get the windows cleaned and gutters cleared out. Make sure you keep up with homeowner's maintenance like touch up painting and chalking, changing air filters regularly, draining the hot water heater to release sediment, etc.

Make sure the utilities have been transferred into your name ahead of time. Some utility companies (like the gas company) require someone to be present if they need to be turned on. So transferring without interruption can save you having to wait around for the gas man.

As a homeowner there are a lot more things to keep an eye on than when you were a tenant. Common homeowner's maintenance is easy and will preserve your property in the long run. Enjoy your new residence and look forward to the years of great memories you will create in this home.

## Refer Your Trusted Advisors

Don't forget to thank the professionals who helped you along the way. The best compliment for a real estate and mortgage professional is a referral. Refer your friends and co-workers to your trusted team of advisors.

**SECRET REVEALED: A referral from a satisfied client is the best compliment a professional can receive.**

Watch Video
http://bit.ly/KluOWq

## Secrets Revealed Recap

1. Change your locks & security alarm codes after closing.

2. A referral from a satisfied client is the best compliment a professional can receive.

## Section III – Real Estate Insider Secrets Revealed

# Chapter 6

## Credit Report Secrets Revealed

Your credit score now affects so many different areas of life, it is crucial to take your score seriously and take steps to improve it. Even if you have great credit, it is still important to take steps to optimize your score. The bottom-line – the higher your score, the better your terms on all kinds of financial products from credit cards to auto loans to insurance and even employment. Your score grades your financial character everywhere.

For the purposes of a home purchase, your score determines whether or not you can obtain traditional financing. The score affects the cost for a home mortgage as well. The challenge is – the score changes all the time and what makes it adjust can be difficult to pin point. This becomes crucial when you apply for a home loan. You may qualify for a certain home loan and when you get closer to closing on your home, your score adjusts down and "boom" you are surprised by a higher cost or even a potential "decline." Not fun.

In the home loan world, credit scores are king. There are minimum required scores to obtain financing. At the time of this writing, the minimum score to obtain an F.H.A. home loan is 580. However, most lenders will not loan F.H.A. unless the score is 620. There are rumors of banks requiring a minimum of 640 scores to fund F.H.A. loans. Minimum scores for conventional loans are set even higher.

**SECRET REVEALED: In the home loan world, credit scores are king.**

## Which Score Do the Mortgage Lenders Use?

Home mortgage lenders will "pull" scores from the big "three" credit bureaus. The scores almost always differ from each other. Mortgage lenders will use the middle score of the borrower. If there is a co-borrower, both will need to qualify. If both are going on the loan, you will take the lowest mid score between the two.

It is best to get your scores from a reputable mortgage lender as scores differ between industries. The scores generated for the auto industry are different than those generated for home loans.

If you know you have credit scores that are well above 740 then you will no doubt be in position to get the best possible financing. However, the majority of Americans don't. So the following information will be helpful. Let's start with a review of the credit reporting industry.

**SECRET REVEALED: Mortgage lenders use the middle score of the three major credit bureaus.**

## Credit

What is a credit report? Simply, it is a detailed history of your willingness to pay. A credit report is a payment history of your revolving (credit cards) and installment (auto, student loan, etc.) accounts provided by a **credit reporting agency**. A local credit reporting agency will pull information from one or all of the three national credit reporting bureaus – **Experian, Trans Union, Equifax (& now a 4ᵗʰ – Innovis)**. Most revolving charge card and installment loan finance companies report a borrower's account payment history to one or all of these national credit-reporting bureaus. Collection accounts, judgments, tax liens, foreclosures, and bankruptcies will also show on the credit report. The credit report will show a monthly breakdown of when and how long an account is or was past due (thirty days, sixty days, ninety days, etc.) It will also show the balances and monthly payments for the accounts. The credit report is a good indication of your "willingness to pay" and is often the deciding factor whether or not a creditor will extend credit.

## How to Establish Credit

Those who have never established any formal credit may find themselves in a dilemma. Credit grantors often won't issue new credit unless the applicant already has credit. Those without credit can find it difficult to show the history of other credit that grantors want to see. To establish a few accounts, a borrower can apply for a **secured credit card**. A secured credit card is where you open a small savings account ($300-$500) with a credit card grantor. The savings account is usually the maximum credit limit and is the security for the credit card should the account not be paid as agreed. Most banks and credit unions also offer installment loans secured by a savings account. Pay the account(s) on time for several months to establish a good credit history. Once the credit history is established, other credit card companies (that don't require savings deposits) will likely grant you credit. Once a history is established, deposits and the savings account will be returned to you. Make sure the credit grantor reports to the national reporting bureaus and make sure the credit grantor is a reputable company. A credit seeker may also find a co-signer for a credit card. A parent or relative may co-sign for a card and the co-signer will be held jointly responsible for the payments. After a few months of paying on time, you may apply for a few more cards in your own name. **Be careful not to go into debt** with this new credit and keep the balances down or paid off so as not to be charged high credit card interest rates.

**SECRET REVEALED: Establish credit with a secured credit card or credit line.**

# Quick Points for Maintaining Good Credit

Paying your credit accounts on time is the primary way of keeping a good credit rating. Keeping your balances low in ratio to the credit limit or paid off each month is important. Optimize the amount and type of credit: two to three credit cards, one installment and one additional account is good. Avoid collection accounts – work with the creditors before it gets to the point of a collection. Keep old credit card accounts open and use them from time to time to keep them active. Do not close old credit card accounts that are in good standing.

**SECRET REVEALED: Don't close credit card accounts that have been open for a long time.**

Do not open multiple new accounts unless you have to and then only a few. Run your credit report at least once a year and review for mistakes. A good way to monitor it is www.AnnualCreditReport.Com and pull one bureau every four months. You are allowed one pull per bureau per year for free. This will also reveal identity theft or credit fraud. Credit reporting software puts the most emphasis on the previous twelve months credit history. Paying off old collections can hurt your score unless they are deleted from your record.

Your credit report and credit rating is as unique as you are. Every credit report is different and most everyone has had times when their credit was bruised. I have helped hundreds of home buyers who thought their credit was shot and come to find out that it was not as bad as they thought. Others I have worked with had to follow a plan to fix their credit so they could be in a position to buy a home.

**SECRET REVEALED: Paying off old collection accounts can hurt your score.**

# Fair Credit

In 1971, Congress passed the Fair Credit Reporting Act (The Law). Its purpose is to set forth guidelines for "fair" and "accurate" credit reporting. Credit reporting agencies are governed by this act and must adhere to its provisions. Penalties to the credit reporting agency and creditor can be severe for non-compliance. The compliance procedures set up by the fair credit reporting act are the key to one being able to "repair" or "clean up" a report rating.

# Credit Reporting Agencies

Credit reporting agencies are in the business of collecting consumer credit information and providing that information, usually for a fee, to grantors of credit (credit card, auto finance, home loan companies, etc.). There are local credit bureaus and national credit bureaus. The three "major" national credit reporting companies are Experian, Equifax, TransUnion and Innovis. Most credit grantors report to one or all the three "majors" (and now a 4th called Innovis). The credit grantors usually submit their customer's account history each month to the "majors." A credit report contains a list of consumer's credit accounts. The date the account was opened, the high credit limit, the amount owing, the minimum monthly payment and history of any late payments or past due balances are included in the credit report. A credit report can be obtained by a potential credit grantor from one or all of the majors (with the consumer's written permission or implied permission, through web applications or over the phone). Or a credit grantor (like a mortgage company) can obtain a credit report from a local credit bureau (agency) who will compile information from the national credit bureaus as well as other sources. The credit grantor will analyze the credit report to make a determination to extend or not extend a consumer a line of credit. A consumer's ability to borrow money can hinge on what is reported on a credit report and the fair credit reporting act was established to ensure "fair and accurate" reporting of information. However, the credit reporting system is not perfect. The sheer volume of information being collected, assimilated, and reported creates common instances of incorrect reporting and/or non-compliance with procedures. This offers the consumer a way to use the law to fix bad credit. Unfortunately, the burden to fix a negative credit report is on the consumer. Credit repair takes time and patience but it is well worth the effort.

## Steps for Correcting a Credit Report

There are ways to correct and repair a credit report by consumers who are willing to put forth the effort. Credit scores now affect so many facets of our financial life it is wise to pursue corrections and repairs if needed. The idea is to get your credit scores raised as far and as fast as possible. It will take work but it is important to you and your financial future.

First, a borrower can obtain a credit report from the "major" credit reporting bureaus: Experian, Equifax, Trans Union (and Innovis). The "majors" will supply a complimentary credit report upon request at www.annualcreditreport.com once a year.

If you request a score, there is a charge.

Experian
NCAC
P.O. Box 9595
Allen, TX 75013
(800) 583-4080 [9:00am-5:00pm In Your Time Zone]
www.consumer.com/consumer/index.html

Equifax
P.O. Box 740256
Atlanta, GA 30374
(800) 797-7033
[9:00am-5:00pm In Your Time Zone]
http://www.econsumer.equifax.com/else

Trans Union
P.O. Box 2000
Chester, PA 19022-2000
(800) 916-8800 [8:30am-4:30pm In Your Time Zone]
www.transunion.com/investigate

Innovis
Attention: Consumer Assistance
P.O. Box 1358
Columbus, OH 43216-1358
www.innovis.com

In my experience, a quicker and more efficient way to obtain a credit report is to apply for a home loan with a local mortgage company who will obtain a "merged" credit report. A local credit bureau will merge info from the three major bureaus (& possibly Innovis). The local credit bureau's report can be easier to read and the bureau is available to explain the report to their client – the mortgage company. The mortgage company can then in turn explain the derogatory items and remedies to you. The local bureau can also be of great help in correcting and re-verifying the credit entries. A mortgage company who has a close working relationship with their credit reporting bureau can be a huge help. The credit bureau can use uncommon knowledge and relationships with both creditors and the "majors" to help clear up a credit report for you through the mortgage company client.

**SECRET REVEALED: Mortgage companies working with local credit bureaus can be a great help.**

The consumer should review the report with the mortgage company and decide what information is incorrect. Ask the mortgage company to ask the bureau to provide all of the creditor's addresses and telephone numbers that are associated with each account entry on the credit report. You may also want the mortgage company to have the credit bureau break up the tri-merged credit report so you can see what each "major" is reporting separately. Almost every credit report has errors. Check names, addresses, social security numbers, etc. Go through every account entry and make a note of items that you know are wrong. Next, go through the report and make a note of account entries that could be wrong or are partially correct. Make a note of all derogatory information that is correct and that you would like to have removed.

# Disputes

A consumer has the right to challenge (dispute) any of the information contained in a credit report. If a consumer believes the information to be inaccurate or obsolete, the credit bureau must investigate the item being challenged. If a borrower has proof (ex. canceled check) of an account being paid, you need to work the problem out with the creditor first then the credit reporting agency can approach the creditor and verify the creditor's records. It is important to present any proof of timely payment and resolve the discrepancy with the creditor who is reporting the error first. The credit bureaus will only change information reported, with the validation of the creditor. The credit bureau is obligated to request verification of information from the creditor and the creditor must provide the proof to the credit bureau within thirty days. If the information is not re-verified by the creditor within the thirty days, the derogatory information must be deleted from the credit report. There is now a fifteen-day extension they can ask for, bringing the investigation time to forty-five days. Information that is accurate but not re-verifiable can also be removed. For instance, if a creditor is no longer in business and can't be contacted for verification – the item can be removed. Items that are out-dated must also be removed.

Items can be deleted from the credit report if seven years have passed since the incident (ten years for bankruptcies). Often, those with common names can have credit items reported that are not theirs. Credit entries that are not the consumers can be removed. If the credit item was discharged in a bankruptcy and still shows past due, it can be removed from the report or it can be changed to a zero balance showing "included in bankruptcy." The dispute must be specific (ex. request the account have the balance and past due made zero). Also, the creditor that is reporting the derogatory information can voluntarily delete the item from the credit report.

A borrower can try to negotiate directly with the creditor to take a partial or full settlement in return for having the account "deleted" from the credit report. Often, a consumer may not even be aware of adverse items until they have been turned down for credit. Being turned down for credit can be discouraging and embarrassing and the consumer is not usually given the procedures for correcting the problem. The consumer must pursue steps to correct and repair the credit so as to not be denied credit in the future.

## SECRET REVEALED: Disputes can help correct or delete derogatory credit entries.

An important note about "Disputes" on credit reports. Recently, F.H.A. has not allowed some home loans to be funded when there were outstanding "disputes" on the credit report. So make sure you work with your mortgage lender and local credit bureau to work through and resolve disputes if you are beginning the process of buying a home.

# Write a Letter to the Bureaus (Eliminate Inaccuracies)

The next step in credit repair is to write a letter to the "major" credit bureaus (Experian, Trans Union, Equifax and now Innovis) and to the local bureau explaining the inaccuracies found on the credit report. If a credit card company is reporting late payments and you have proof the payments were made on time, you will also want to send a letter to each of the creditors that have reported inaccurately. Include copies of any documentation that will back your explanations (canceled checks, divorce decree, closing statements, etc.). Send your letters "Certified" return receipt requested.

Often times, after a bankruptcy, credit that was discharged in the bankruptcy still shows on the credit as being delinquent. Provide a copy of the bankruptcy discharge papers showing that the account was included in the bankruptcy. Ask that each derogatory statement be re-verified for accuracy. Remember, at your request, the credit bureau must contact each creditor for verification of derogatory information. If re-verification from the creditor is not received within thirty days, the account must be legally stricken from your report. Even derogatory credit that is reported correctly can be removed if the procedures are not followed as set out by law. This is how many of the so-called "credit repair companies" use the system to remove unwanted credit blemishes. They send letters month after month to credit bureaus hoping that the creditor or bureau will fail to respond to disputes within thirty days or that the creditor decides it is not worth the time and paperwork to continue to update the reported information. The consumer can use that process to try to remove unwanted items, however, it is not fool proof as some creditors will be relentless in following the verification procedures. Even if only a few unwanted credit blemishes are removed, it will be well worth the effort. This method can also be used with those with good credit to present a clear and "correct" credit report to anyone who sees it.

**SECRET REVEALED: Simple corrections can raise your score.**

# Negotiate with Creditors

Negotiating with creditors is sometimes the easiest and quickest way to fix credit. Most creditors or collection agencies don't want to ruin someone's credit – they just want to be paid. A consumer who wants to clear the blemish from the credit may simply just ask. For instance, if a dentist has placed a collection account on a consumer's credit report for an unpaid bill, the consumer can contact the dentist and negotiate a payment plan or offer to pay off the collection account in return for the account being "deleted" from the credit report completely. The collector may even settle for a percentage of the total amount owed. Even if the creditor demands the full amount, ask that the account be "deleted" when it is paid. Collection accounts that have been paid will still show on a credit report as "paid collection accounts" or "paid charge offs" and are still considered derogatory, and this does not help the score. Settling a collection account can drive the score lower, if the agency is not willing to delete. Accounts that are "deleted" are removed completely from the report and it is as if the incident never happened. Do not pay off an account unless the creditor acknowledges in writing that the account will show as deleted or at least "paid." Paying a collection agency may not help the score, it may actually hurt your score. If you do decide to pay it off, then at least it will keep the agency from sending the account to another agency later on. Paying or settling an account with the original creditor, not to be confused with a collection agency, will always help the score and prevent the account from being sent or sold to a collection agency.

**SECRET REVEALED: Getting derogatory accounts deleted is like the event never happened.**

A very complete "paper trail" should be established. Some local credit bureaus will allow you to pay the bill through the credit bureau so the item can be removed from the report immediately. When negotiating with a creditor, ask to speak to the credit manager or supervisor. There is no use wasting time talking with someone who does not have the authority to make decisions regarding a credit issue. Keep a log showing the date and time of the calls, and document what was discussed and who was spoken to. It may take several calls and letters to resolve the issue, but it is worth the effort. It doesn't hurt to mention the Fair Credit Reporting Act and even potential legal action in the letter.

There are even cases where "correct" derogatory credit can be removed by pleading with the creditor to remove it. A creditor may value a consumer's account enough to remove the blemishes as a sign of good faith.

## The Credit Bureaus Rights

The Fair Credit Reporting Act allows credit bureaus to refuse to investigate items that are considered "frivolous" or "irrelevant." It is up to the credit bureaus to decide what requests are "frivolous or irrelevant." A letter that is sent to the bureau claiming "everything is wrong" stands a good chance of being considered "frivolous" and the bureau may refuse to reinvestigate.

## Credit Report Explanations (Statements)

If all else fails in removing derogatory entries from a report, the Fair Credit Reporting Act gives the right to the consumer to include a statement of up to one hundred words telling the consumer's side of the story. The statement will be printed out on the credit report every time it is run by a creditor although it won't help the credit score.

## Inquiries

Every time a credit report is run it will create an inquiry. An inquiry will show which creditor ran a credit report and when. A common misunderstanding about inquiries is that they can hurt the score. The scores have been designed to allow multiple inquiries within a thirty-day period for financing inquiries. You can have your credit pulled as many times as necessary, within a thirty-day period, when shopping for rates, and the inquiries for each industry will only count as one inquiry against your score.

However, too many inquiries on a credit report from different trade types can affect the credit rating. You don't want to apply for a credit card then an auto loan then a credit line and then a home mortgage. This will hurt your score.

**SECRET REVEALED: Multiple inquiries in a thirty-day period in the same industry has a very minor effect on the score.**

## Do Not Close Long Standing Accounts

The credit reporting software looks at how long an account has been open and if it has a small balance, it will give you credit for the long history. If you pay the account off, it will have a little effect. Keeping older credit card accounts active will always help the scores. Don't pay off an older account to open a new account. This will almost always drop the score.

## Balances on Credit Cards

The score software counts balances on credit cards as a very high percentage of your score. It is always advisable to keep balances under 19% of the credit limit. Scores work on a percentage basis. If you go over 19%, this will negatively affect your score. If you go over 39%, 59%, 79% and 99%, it will negatively affect your score with each higher percentage. Your best bet is to keep your balances under 19% of the credit limit even if you have to redistribute balances across different cards to do so.

**SECRET REVEALED: Keep credit card balances under 19% of the credit limit.**

Another thing to watch out for is when credit card companies lower your credit limit. Lately, credit card issuers have been lowering available credit limits at their own discretion. You may have had a good balance to limit ratio with a $1,900 balance and a $10,000 limit and the credit card issuer lowers you limit to $3,500 – now your ratio exceeds 50%.

**SECRET REVEALED: Watch out for your credit card companies lowering your credit limit.**

## Number of Credit Card Accounts

The best score is obtained by only having two to three revolving accounts and one installment account. You can lose points when you go over three, four, etc. Go over seven and you will get hit real hard. The scoring software also looks at how long you have had credit established and if you have a long credit history, your score will not be affected as much by the number of accounts than if you have opened a bunch of new accounts with a short history.

**SECRET REVEALED: Optimize your credit with the proper mix of accounts.**

## Different Scores For Different Industries

Always keep in mind that each industry score is different. An automotive score is different from a credit card score. If you purchase the scores from websites offering scores, they will in most cases not be reliable for a mortgage. It can be used as a barometer for those, working on fixing their credit report to see a before and after effect. Each industry also has their own scale for what they consider an acceptable score for different rates. An exceptional score for a mortgage might be 740, but for the auto industry it might be 840. The scoring scale is completely different for different industries.

# No Credit is Not Good Credit

Unfortunately, those who like to pay cash for everything can have a problem getting a score generated. This does not seem fair but it happens all the time, especially to immigrants who moved here from out of the country. They don't have a credit history here in the U.S. and therefore no score. It is wise to establish credit early in the game and keep your payments in good standing and your balance to limit ratios low.

# Credit Repair Agencies

People have been scammed out of hundreds and even thousands of dollars by unscrupulous organizations that promise better credit and then don't deliver. There are credit repair companies that do a fair to good job and help get scores up but "beware" – the scammers are out there. Beware of organizations that seem to be legit but can actually prolong or further damage credit scores. So-called "credit counseling services" that can actually be collection agencies in disguise. I have worked with clients time and time again that went to "counseling" agencies and the situation turned out to be a nightmare. Some of them tell you to stop making payments so the creditors will negotiate with you – bad advice. Debt consolidation companies can be counted as bad as bankruptcy on credit reports for mortgage purposes.

**SECRET REVEALED: Be very careful about using so-called credit counseling services and credit repair companies.**

Because of the abuse of credit repair agencies in the past, a law was passed. "The Credit Repair Organizations Act" sets out strict guidelines for credit repair organizations. You can find these guidelines on the Federal Trade Commission's website: www.ftc.gov.

Before signing up with a credit repair agency, I suggest you review the contract. The law spells out what must be followed by credit repair agencies, including a three day right of rescission to cancel a contract and a full written description of what the credit repair company will do for you and when.

The credit repair process is something you can do on your own. It is not necessary to pay for services. Consider free credit repair.

There are several organizations that have been set up to help consumers get their credit in order without payment. Even some national builders have stepped up to help home buyers out and provide free credit repair. Obviously, the builder hopes that you will purchase one of their homes but it is not a requirement of the program that you purchase a home from the builder.

Watch Video
http://bit.ly/NvQj7C

# Secrets Revealed Recap

1. In the home loan world, credit scores are king.

2. Mortgage lenders use the middle score of the three major credit bureaus.

3. Establish credit with a secured credit card or credit line.

4. Don't close credit card accounts that have been open for a long time.

5. Paying off old collection accounts can hurt your score.

6. Mortgage companies working with local credit bureaus can be a great help.

7. Disputes can help correct or delete derogatory credit entries.

8. Simple corrections can raise your score.

9. Getting derogatory accounts deleted is like the event never happened.

10. Multiple inquiries in a thirty-day period in the same industry has a very minor effect on the score.

11. Keep credit card balances under 19% of the credit limit.

12. Watch out for your credit card companies lowering your credit limit.

13. Optimize your credit with the proper mix of accounts.

14. Be very careful about using so-called credit counseling services and credit repair companies.

# Chapter 7

## Home Loan Secrets Revealed

In recent years, the home mortgage industry has undergone dramatic changes. An economic crisis that was created by a mortgage industry gone wild. Too much easy money led to too many people buying houses who should not have been buying in the first place. Speculators bought homes with the expectation of never ending price increases. Irresponsible buying and lending practices led to foreclosures across the country on home loans that should have never been funded. The fall out from this has been the failure or bail out of major players in the formerly irrationally exuberant mortgage landscape. This has led to reform in the way home loans are underwritten and approved.

The underwriting guidelines are consistently being re-written to try to prevent the problem that was created by too much easy money. And this is a good thing. The challenge is that the guidelines keep changing faster than anyone but an expert can keep up with. I am in constant contact with my trusted home loan expert because the guideline changes happen quickly and often. Having been a mortgage company owner myself, I once knew the guidelines backward & forward. Now I have to keep up with the changes by constantly getting updates from the experts in the "trenches" in the new home mortgage market.

117

**SECRET REVEALED: Guidelines change often – work with a mortgage expert.**

The good news is that the new guidelines are meant to keep us <u>in</u> our homes rather than giving them back to the bank. Although the guidelines are stricter than they were a few years ago, they are more in line with the "normal" guidelines we had before the easy, greasy lending standards began.

# Feds Help First Timers

The great news is that the government realized how important first time homebuyers are to the economy and have made it attractive and easier to get financing by offering tax credits and incentives to first time homebuyers. Loans for first timers are available and insured by the government. The Federal Housing Administration (F.H.A.) now insures over 30% of home mortgages nationally. A majority of first timers use F.H.A. financing which allows for a 3.5% down payment and expanded underwriting criteria. It allows those with less than stellar credit to qualify for a home. This does not mean you can have absolutely terrible credit and no job but it does mean that those with documentable income, a small down payment, and fairly good credit can get into a home.

**SECRET REVEALED: Buyers with a job, a small down payment, and reasonably good credit can get a loan.**

At the time of this writing, the National Association of Realtors reported that 53% of homes being purchased in the U.S. were first time homebuyers. This has been largely due to a buyer's market and their ability to obtain financing with the help of F.H.A. and other government programs. First timers are taking advantage of bank owned homes and homebuilders who are willing to "bargain." It is a great time to be a first time homebuyer.

Although some segments of the mortgage loan products (subprime & EZ qualifier) have evaporated, the truth is that there are still great options for first time homebuyers. One of the great myths media perpetuates is that "banks are not lending." That is completely false. How they lend has changed. The majority of homes being sold today are to first timers.

**SECRET REVEALED: The majority of home sales in America are to first time home buyers.**

# Cost of Getting Into a Home

## Down payment, closing costs, & prepaid expenses

The minimum down payment for most home buyers is 0% to 3.5% down. The average closing costs on a purchase are 2-3% of the sales price and the prepaid expenses are 1-2% of the sales price. Some closing costs and prepaid items can be financed into the interest rate or possibly paid by the seller or builder. Closing costs are those fees that are charged to a buyer for services rendered in accommodating the closing (lender, title, etc.) Prepaid expenses are pro-rations for taxes, insurance, and interest.

**SECRET REVEALED: Having the seller pay closing costs can cut the cash needed to close in half.**

# Types of Loan Programs

The majority of first time loans are government backed or government insured. A few examples of minimum down payment home loan products that you may be discussing with your loan officer are:

1.    F.H.A. Insured Mortgage – F.H.A. is a 3.5% down payment home loan product (most first timers use F.H.A.)

2.       V.A. Zero Down Guaranteed loan for Veterans and Active duty
3.       USDA Zero Down for rural and semi-rural properties
4.       Government sponsored bond financing

# Government Loans

Government loan programs are those that are insured or guaranteed by the federal government such as F.H.A. (Federal Housing Administration) and V.A. (Veterans Administration) for those qualified military personnel & veterans. Conforming loans are those that conform to the FNMA or FHLMC (Fannie Mae, Freddie Mac) guidelines. Fannie Mae and Freddie Mac are now owned by the government so they are also considered to be "backed" by the federal government. Conforming loans require down payments of 5%-20% or more. Loans less than 20% down require additional premiums for private mortgage insurance or PMI. It is important to have your loan officer show you a comparison between F.H.A., VA, USDA, and FNMA & FHLMC conforming loans to help you decide which loan is best for you.

**SECRET REVEALED: Most home loans are backed by the federal government.**

# Other Loan Programs

**Portfolio Loans** – A portfolio loan is a loan that is not sold to or insured by the government but held in a lender's portfolio. The lender will "hold" the loan and collect payments until it is paid off. The nice thing about portfolio loans is that the lender is able to step outside the guidelines that government loans require. Because of the flexibility, portfolio loans can carry a higher interest rate and different loan terms. Portfolio lenders are not a huge segment of the market and can be found at local banks and credit unions.

**SECRET REVEALED: Portfolio loans can be found at local banks and credit unions.**

**Sub-Prime** – As of the time of this writing, the sub-prime loan market has all but evaporated. Years of irresponsible lending led to one of our nation's worst financial crisis's. Sub-prime loans will make a slow come back but will be much more limited and conservative – for good reason. So, for those with sub-prime credit, the best advise is to take the steps to improve your credit so you can qualify for an F.H.A. or other government backed loan.

**SECRET REVEALED: Subprime loans are all but gone (for good reason).**

# Private Money and Cash

Emerging now to help fill the gap that sub-prime left behind is private money. These are loans that are offered by individual investors who lend on real estate. Although it is a small segment of the market, private money is becoming more available. A larger down payment is required and higher interest rates are charged. Like portfolio lenders, the private lender can make their own underwriting decisions and don't have to conform to government lending rules. In some cases, a parent or relative can become the private money lender where they can get better yields on real estate than leaving it in the bank. I've recently experienced several parents step in and pay cash for their kid's first home.

**SECRET REVEALED: You may have a relative who will loan you the funds to buy a home.**

# Types of Lenders

A top tier lender will know the program guidelines and how to best direct you to the home loan product that will best fit your needs. Also, a top tier lender will charge a fair and equitable interest rate and fees. There are several different types of lending companies and all have their advantages and disadvantages. Here are some examples of lending company types as explained by mortgage expert Kenton Brown, V.P. of Sente Mortgage:

The three most common places to currently obtain funds for your house are as follows:

1.    Banks
2.    Mortgage Brokers
3.    Mortgage Bankers

**The Bank** – The "big banks" are the primary source of capital available for all home mortgage financing. Currently, there are three big banks in the United States and they have similar offers to each other. There are also many private banks and credit unions which can be an excellent source for mortgage financing. Customers walk in the front door as a "retail" customer and they can request to speak to a mortgage loan officer. Unfortunately, they may refer you to an 800 number where you will not get the best service.

The main advantage is that they are the primary source of capital available in the marketplace today. Primary disadvantages are that they are rather large institutions and sometimes the consumer can get tied up in "red tape" and will not be able to close their transaction timely. Also, they have one product line and cannot "shop" around for the best terms for the consumer. They offer what they offer and that is it. Furthermore, they can also sometimes lack expertise as they are generally not as experienced as other seasoned loan professionals. They can be challenged as they offer a wide variety of products and it is difficult to be a "jack of all trades" and master of none. (Insurance, financial planning, car loans, boat loans, home loans.)

On the other end of the spectrum is the **mortgage broker.** A few years ago, the represented 60% of all mortgage transactions in the marketplace. The Sub-prime crisis of 2007 changed this drastically. These are generally smaller companies that sell loans to larger institutions. The big advantage is that they can deal with many different banks and "shop" around for the programs for the consumer. Their main disadvantage is that they usually can't control the transaction completely throughout the process. They meet with the customer and collect all of their paperwork, but then send the loan to the investor and have to sometimes deal with unpredictable results from underwriting (those that approve the loans). They also sometimes lose control as those investors must close the loan as well and depending on volume demands, may not be able to execute timely. These two things can be very frustrating for the consumer. Mortgage brokers currently represent only 15% of all loans currently being done in the market place.

The third way to finance a home is with a **mortgage banker.** This is sometimes confused with a mortgage broker as they can "shop" with several different investors and obtain the best rates for the consumer, but there is one fundamental difference and it all boils down to control. Since the mortgage banker can use their own funds to fund transactions, they are able to meet with the customer, gather and process the paperwork, underwrite, approve and close the loan all under one roof. This allows more predictable results for the consumer and usually allows them to be communicated with more effectively as well as close timely with minimal hassle. Also, they are usually smaller to medium sized companies and provide higher levels of individualized service.

## Probing Questions to Ask Your Lender

The following questions will help qualify your lenders. They will also imply that you know how their business works which sets a professional tone:

1.  How long has the loan officer been in the lending business? (I consider at least five years or longer to be good.)

2. What was their loan volume last year? (I feel that a good loan officer working full-time should fund at least $400,000-500,000 per month or at least $5 to $6 million per year.)
3. Are they a banker or a broker? A banker has their own money to lend; a broker uses other banking funds to close loans. Some bankers can also broker mortgages to other banks.
4. Are they F.H.A. direct endorsed lenders? This means they have underwriting approval power for F.H.A. loans.
5. Ask them how the bond market is doing today. (This is a common industry "insider" question because as the bond market moves up or down, so do mortgage rates. If they don't follow the bond market, they probably are not a serious lender.)
6. Ask them to give the names and phone numbers of the last three clients they funded a loan for and ask if you can check those references.

## Interest Rate Locks

Discuss with your lender the interest rate lock policy. In most cases, you will have to have found a property before you can lock an interest rate. Rates are usually locked for sixty days or less. Extended locks can be requested but may involve an up front "lock fee." Keep in mind that interest rates fluctuate daily and that you can follow the rate moves by following the yields on the ten and thirty year Treasury Bonds. The bond yields usually move in the same direction as mortgage interest rates. If you are getting close to closing on a home, you may want to check rates daily with your lender. If rates look like they are taking a turn for the worse, you may want to lock in. Ask your lender if they provide a float down. This can be very helpful as you can lock a rate and if rates get substantially better, then your lender can offer to "float down" your rate to the current going rate.

**SECRET REVEALED: Follow the ten and thirty year treasury bond yields to help determine where rates are headed.**

# What Lenders Look At

There are four main areas that lenders evaluate when reviewing your loan application. They are:

1. Employment/Income
2. Assets
3. Liabilities/Credit
4. The Property

# Employment

Home mortgage lenders look at a borrower's income, employment, job stability, and whether a borrower is self-employed or salaried. Self-employed borrowers are qualified differently than salaried borrowers. Salaried borrowers are those who have a set pay and include hourly employees. They are usually paid a set amount at regular intervals and are issued a W-2 form at the end of the year. On the other hand, self-employed individuals include commissioned employees and those that own more than 20% of their company. They are issued a 1099 and/or file a schedule "C" or corporate tax returns. Underwriting guidelines for salaried employees are different than for self-employed borrowers.

# Income

Lenders are looking for a two-year history of employment. They prefer to see you in the same line of work or type of work for the past two years. If you just got out of college or trade school, lenders will consider your degree or training in lieu of having a two-year employment history. Lenders will figure your qualifying income from the base salary. They will average your bonuses, overtime, & commissions over the past two years. You will most likely provide two years of W2s and possibly two years of tax returns if you are an employed worker. The computerized underwriting system may only ask for one year of income documentation or it could ask for three years. This is why it is important for you to get pre-approved and have your lender "run it through the system" (computerized underwriter) and see what the "system" requires for your income documentation. I have experienced many times where the system has approved a home loan based on only one year's income, which made the difference for my customer getting the home. If you switch jobs, the lender will probably want one month of pay stubs from the new job even if it is the same line of work. Don't quit your salaried job or go self-employed while you are in the home buying process.

**SECRET REVEALED: Have your lender run your loan file "through the system" – (computerized underwriter).**

# Self-Employed

Self-employed, commissioned, or contract workers are treated very differently than salaried employees. With a salaried employee, their income can be counted almost immediately to qualify for a home based on the current gross salary. For self-employed people, income calculations are based on a two-year average of the "net" income after all expenses. Needless to say, new businesses have a tendency to "net" less during the first few years of operation and this can affect what a self-employed person can qualify for. Commissioned sales, contract employees, and temp workers all need a two-year history and their income will be based on their average net income after expenses.

**SECRET REVEALED: Salaried buyers are qualified on gross income. Self-employed are qualified on the "net."**

The averaging of the net and the two-year requirement surprises and disappoints many self-employed home buyers. If you are a salaried borrower and plan to become self-employed –

buy a home before you quit your salaried job. A salaried borrower who has become self-employed will have to wait two years to qualify for a standard loan. A self-employed borrower can go back to work on salary in the same line of work and will qualify when their first paycheck is received.

As with any rule, there are exceptions, so it is best to consult with your trusted lending professional to get the answers.

**SECRET REVEALED: Buy the home before you become self-employed.**

# Cosigners

Cosigners can help a home buyer who needs more qualifying power. The co-borrowers income and debts are combined with the borrowers and is averaged out. F.H.A. allows non-occupant co-borrowers to co-sign and this allows for those buyers who need help (or may not even have income like college students) to qualify to purchase a home. Co-signers do not cancel out or average out bad credit, however. If you have low credit scores, you will benefit by following the techniques covered in the "credit report secrets" chapter.

**SECRET REVEALED: F.H.A. allows for non-occupant co-signers, which is perfect for college student home buyers.**

# Assets/Cash to Close

The total cash to close will include the down payment (if any), closing costs (fees paid to those who assist you in acquiring the home loan) and prepaid expenses (prorations and reserves for taxes & insurance). The cash to purchase the home can come from any number of sources. Common sources for cash to close are savings or borrowing the cash from a 401k plan. An employer may allow up to half or more of the balance of a 401k to be borrowed and the employee will pay the loan back to the 401k plan through small payroll deductions.

New tax laws allow first time homebuyer's (defined as those who have not owned a home in the past three years) to liquidate up to $10,000 of an IRA, penalty free. Even relatives can cash in IRA's penalty free to help the buyer with the cash to close (check w/CPA). The cash to close can come from a relative in the form of a gift. There are specific rules and procedures that need to be followed if receiving a gift. The gift has to be documented very carefully and a gift letter will need to accompany the gift.

Some creative sources of funds to close can be the seller, the lender, and even the real estate professional. A seller is allowed to pay 3% or more of the sales price towards a buyer's closing costs. This simple provision (seller paid closing costs) written into the purchase agreement can cut the cash to close in half. A lender can also assist with cash to close by financing closing costs into the interest rate. A small increase in the interest rate can cover thousands of dollars of up-front money. The higher the interest rate, the more closing costs a lender can cover for the borrower. In certain cases, even the real estate professional can assist with closing costs using part of their commission to help out.

A secured loan can also be a source for down payment. Some government organizations have down payment assistance programs available. A source of funds that are usually "not" allowed is "mattress money." Money that is kept at home or in a safe deposit box cannot be counted for closing because it is untraceable and the lender will assume that the funds are coming from an unsecured loan or some other un-allowed sources. If you have "mattress money," cash not in a bank account, it would be wise to deposit the money in the bank several months prior to applying for a home loan to allow the money to "season." Whatever the source of the funds, thorough documentation and "paper trails" are very important.

**SECRET REVEALED: The builder, seller, lender, and even the real estate agent can contribute to a buyer's "cash to close."**

# Liabilities

An area that lenders analyze very closely is the liabilities and credit history. The lender will look at installment debt payments (auto, student loans, etc.) and revolving charge card's minimum monthly payments. Child support, alimony, and childcare costs are also counted in monthly debt. A lender will allow approximately 42% (and in some cases, up to 50%) of the gross monthly income to be committed to all of the borrower's debt including the home payment. To determine how much of a home loan you can qualify for, multiply your gross monthly income by .42 (or 42%). Then subtract out your other monthly debts. That figure is what is left over for a home payment. To qualify for more of a home loan, a borrower may have to rearrange the debt or pay down some balances. For instance, installment loans that are paid down to a balance of less than ten months may not be counted against you. Paying off a $300 car payment could increase your home buying power by more than $30,000! For qualifying purposes, the lender does not count utility expenses or car insurance.

A credit report will be ordered showing your credit history for the last seven to ten years and longer. Credit reports show a fairly accurate history of a borrower's willingness to pay. A credit report can make or break your chances of getting a home loan. There are four major national repositories of credit information – they are Experian, Trans-Union, Equifax (and now a new one called Innovis). The bureaus also check for judgments, foreclosures, bankruptcies, tax liens, and collection accounts. The information will be assimilated into a full "standard factual" credit report for the lender's review. Credit reports often have to be corrected to reflect accurate information. Unfortunately, it is up to the borrower to have information that is contained in the credit report to be researched and corrected if necessary.

Credit criteria for the granting of home loans is different than that of car loans and credit card grantors. In many ways it is easier to qualify for a home loan than other types of credit.

Lenders look closely at the past twelve months of credit history. For instance, a borrower who went bankrupt just two years ago can apply for a home loan if credit has been re-established and there have been no late payments since the bankruptcy. For in-depth information on credit, refer to the chapter "Credit Report Secrets."

## The Property

An appraisal of the property is ordered by the lender to determine the fair market value of the home. Since the home is the collateral for the loan, the lender analyzes the appraisal carefully. An appraiser compares recently sold homes to the one you are buying and assimilates the information into an appraisal report that will show fair market value. In the few cases where the value is less than the sales price, the buyer can try to re-negotiate the price, pay the difference, or possibly back out of the purchase agreement. The appraiser may also require repairs to be completed to the property. Other inspections will be ordered as a part of purchasing. The property inspection is very thorough and it would be wise for a buyer to attend it as a great deal can be learned about the home as the inspector goes through it.

Watch Video
http://bit.ly/MHUtbb

# Secrets Revealed Recap

1. Guidelines change often – work with a mortgage expert.

2. Buyers with a job, a small down payment, and reasonably good credit can get a loan.

3. The majority of home sales in America are to first time home buyers.

4. Having the seller pay closing costs can cut the cash needed to close in half.

5. Most home loans are backed by the federal government.

6. Portfolio loans can be found at local banks and credit unions.

7. Subprime loans are all but gone (for good reason).

8. You may have a relative who will loan you the funds to buy a home.

9. Follow the ten and thirty year treasury bond yield to help determine where rates are headed.

10. Have your lender run your loan file "through the system" – (computerized underwriter).

11. Salaried buyers are qualified on gross income. Self employed are qualified on the "net."

12. Buy the home before you become self-employed.

13. F.H.A. allows for non-occupant co-signers, which is perfect for college student home buyers.

14. The builder, seller, lender, and even the real estate agent can contribute to a buyer's "cash to close."

# Chapter 8

## Home Builder Secrets Revealed

Homebuilding is a huge economic force. Even in tougher times, hundreds of thousands of homes are built each year by private builders, small home building companies and large "production" builders. The majority of homes built in America are built by large production builders. Production home builders are public or privately owned enterprises that construct new homes across the nation to accommodate the rising population and immigration.

Homebuilding is one of the largest industries in the U.S. employing hundreds of thousands of workers from laborers & construction to sales & marketing to top executives.

The industry also supports numerous other industries from lumber and building materials to appliance makers and landscapers. An average home contains over 250,000 individual parts – each having to be manufactured and assembled together to ultimately produce a home.

From raw materials to finished homes, millions of workers are dependent directly or indirectly on homebuilding. As important as the homebuilding industry is to the economy, it is completely dependent on home buyers and home sales to survive and thrive. According to the National Association of Realtors, nearly one third of the home buying market are first time homebuyers. First time homebuyers are a huge economic force. Every time a new home is sold there is an economic ripple effect that rolls through the economy. From paying the salaries of all the industry workers to all the additional products that are purchased by new home buyers such as: appliances, lawn care, gardening equipment, garage door openers, ceiling fans and window coverings. It is no wonder the U.S. government is doing what it can to stimulate first timers to buy.

Most of the national homebuilders produce a good product at a reasonable price. It is a highly competitive industry and margins are small. Some builders build a better product than others. Some use better materials and workmanship and use their volume buying power to help keep their cost down.

The largest home building companies in America are publicly traded companies. They are listed on the New York Stoke Exchange or the NASDAQ. At the time of this writing, the top four builders in terms of number of closed home sales are:

1. Pulte/Centex Homes
2. DR Horton Homes
3. Lennar Corp
4. KB Home

## Home Builders By the Numbers

Most first time home buyers purchase from large national or local volume home builders. These builders are corporations that rely on their reported financial statements to reflect their ongoing performance as a company. It's all about "the numbers." The monthly, quarterly, and yearly "numbers." Knowing this can put you in a better negotiating position. There are "better" times of year to buy from builders. For instance, a builder who is trying to meet a quota before fiscal year end may take a deep discount on a home or even a loss to make up in "volume." A knowledgeable real estate professional will know (or find out) when the fiscal year end is. Also, certain homes will be offered at deeper discounts than others.

**SECRET REVEALED: You can get a great deal on a home when builders are trying to "meet the numbers."**

## Inventory Homes

Another good case for negotiation and great deals is for what are called "aging specs." Spec homes (a.k.a. inventory homes) are homes built as inventory – without a particular home buyer in mind. The reason builders build spec homes is so they have homes available for a buyer who doesn't have the time to go through the building process. For a builder, the problem comes when the spec home sits finished for too long. Week after week, month after month, the unsold home becomes a burden to the builder. So often times you can get a great deal on an "aging spec" because the builder just needs to get rid of it. Their loss can be your gain – big time!

**SECRET REVEALED: Builder spec homes (inventory homes) can be a great deal.**

## Do Your Homework

There are good builders and there are ones you want to stay away from. You need to do your homework when buying from a new home builder. You can do research on the internet, check blogs, etc. Better yet, hire your own experienced buyer's agent who knows builder quality, customer service, and track records.

## Check with the Neighbors

In addition to having good representation, one grass roots way to check on a builder's performance is to knock on a few doors in the neighborhood. Ask a few neighbors how their experience went. Were they satisfied and happy with the process and the final product? Ask how the builder performed on warranty service, etc. Homeowners are usually candid about their experience. But make sure you check with more than one because some homeowners may have had an isolated bad experience or are just plain hard to please. Regardless, if you find a pattern of homeowners who are happy, great! If the majority are dissatisfied then that should raise red flags.

## Reserve the Right to be Represented

When dealing with builders, it is very important to have your own representation. Even if you do start looking at advertisements, billboards, and builder internet sites – make sure you reserve the right to have professional representation. If you wander into a builder's model you will meet the builders representative – the builder's on-site sales agent. Inform the on-site sales agent that you <u>will</u> be having your own representation (even if you have not selected a buyer's agent yet). Keep in mind that builder's on-site sales agents are employees for the builder. As nice as they may be, they are trained sales people who have the builder's best interest (and profit margin) in mind. Just tell the on-site agent that your agent is not with you today but will be with you later.

When you tell the builder's on-site sales agent that you will be having a respected real estate professional representing you they will usually treat you <u>better</u> than if you say you are working alone. In some areas of the nation, builders do not "cooperate" with real estate professionals (meaning pay their fee) but in most areas, builders do cooperate and highly value their relationships with real estate professionals. In my city, up to 80% of new homes are sold by real estate agents. In most cases, builders <u>will not</u> lower the price of the home if you don't have a real estate agent representing you. Some buyers "go it alone" thinking they will get a better deal if they don't have a real estate agent because the builder doesn't have to pay a commission, this is not so. Builders value real estate professionals because they can generate multiple sales each year, whereas you may only buy one home in a lifetime. A top producing real estate agent may sell a dozen or more homes every year.

**SECRET REVEALED: Builders treat buyers better if they have an agent.**

If real estate agents find out that builders are giving discounts to those buyers not having real estate agent representation, they stand to lose the 80% of sales real estate professionals bring to them each year. I heard one builder division president say at a sales meeting that he would "fire an on-site agent on the spot" if they offered deeper discounts to buyers who don't have a real estate agent. So in dealing with a home builder, you have the right "and" the advantage of having your trusted real estate professional negotiate on your behalf.

**SECRET REVEALED: Builders won't discount a home by the commission amount if you don't have an agent.**

If you find a home you like being offered by a builder, you will want to make sure your real estate professional is with you to help you write the purchase agreement. If they are not with you, call them up and tell them you need their help – now. The purchase agreement is usually done at the builder's model or on-site sales office. Most builders negotiate. Even when the on-site sales agent says this is the "bottom line" price – usually it is not. As nice as the on-site sales agent is and as much authority as they portray, they do not make decisions on whether your offer will be accepted. It is always the sales manager back at the main office who decides whether or not your offer will be accepted.

**SECRET REVEALED: On-site sales agents do not make the final pricing decision on a home.**

Now there are times (in hot seller's markets) where there is very little negotiating. But in normal markets and buyer's markets, there is almost always room for negotiation. One thing you have to be careful of is offering too low. Often times, offers that are really low (called low ball) are not taken seriously and you end up not getting a good response from the builder. Sometimes builders will reject the offer that is too low or respond with a minimal adjustment. If you make a reasonably low offer they may just take it. The intention is to get to the <u>sales manager's</u> bottom line or as close to it as possible and this takes a good negotiator.

**SECRET REVEALED: Almost all builders negotiate price & terms.**

Some strategies for getting a lower price may be in seller's concessions such as free upgrades or additional mortgage loan costs paid by the builder. Sometimes a builder is stuck on a price but may throw in a refrigerator or washer & dryer to make you happy. A saying I learned a long time ago in real estate: "if you don't ask, you don't get." So make sure you and your real estate professional ask for everything the builder may be willing to give.

# Neighborhoods are Built in Phases

The large production builders build neighborhoods divided into sections called tracts. These tracts are small or large parcels of land that are subdivided and developed. Land developers put in streets and utilities, water and wastewater drainage. The developer may also put in amenities like golf courses, recreation centers, and pools, etc. Many of the large neighborhoods that are developed nowadays are master planned communities or planned unit developments (P.U.D.s). They can range from several dozen acres to several thousand acres. Some master planned communities can take ten or even twenty years for complete build out. These big communities are developed in "phases." Phasing allows for the neighborhood to be developed in an orderly fashion and keep costs down. A typical tract neighborhood will have one builder or several builders selling homes in conjunction and in competition with each other.

## Best Phase to Buy

The best times to buy during the build out of a neighborhood are at the beginning and at the end of development phases. When developers begin a community, home buyers have a hard time "picturing" a neighborhood. All they can see is a proposed plan and empty lots. Builders will often offer special "pre-construction prices." They will offer below market home prices to spur sales and encourage buyers who can't "see" a neighborhood because it isn't there yet. As builders move through phases of development, they tend to increase the price of homes from phase to phase. This has the effect of increasing the value of the homes in the neighborhood, especially those purchased in the pre-construction phase.

**SECRET REVEALED: The best time to buy is during the beginning and the end of a phase.**

## Close Out Specials

At the end of a building phase or at the ending of development of a neighborhood, builders will often offer close out specials on their remaining inventory. Sometimes they will even take a loss on a home just to be able to "close out" and move their crews & sales agents to the next neighborhood.

**SECRET REVEALED: Check out previous phases to see how the neighborhood is "holding up."**

## Model Homes

On your first visit to a new home, you will arrive at the model home or a model home "park" where there are multiple builders selling new homes. The model homes are usually beautifully decorated and landscaped versions of the builder's product located on the best and most convenient lots. The model homes are usually incredibly "staged" by professional decorators and highly upgraded with all the best (expensive) amenities the builder has to offer. It is important to know that the builder's model home can easily include $50,000 to $100,000 in "upgrades" like granite counters and outdoor living areas that are not "standard" in the builder's base price of the home. Keep a prudent perspective. Understand that what you will end up with will most likely be a more modest version of the "model" home.

Although the builder's model can look like something out of *Better Homes and Gardens*, keep in mind that the "upgrades" that are presented in a model home are some of the biggest sources of hidden profit for the builder. My suggestion is don't fall in love with the model home just because it has wall to wall imported "Brazilian" hard wood floors. As a first home, you will likely choose more modest appointments.

**SECRET REVEALED: Don't fall in love with "model home" decorating and upgrades.**

# The Home Building Process

The new home purchase process differs from the resale home process. Building a home from scratch will take from four to six months or longer from start to finish. You will also be involved in a lot more decisions about how the home comes together.  Building a home can be a lot of fun, but it stretches the stress out over a longer period of time. Building is not a perfect science. As rewarding as the finished product can be – be prepared for some challenges. One great thing about building a home is you are involved in making the house "come together." You will get to choose the lot, the elevation (the way the home looks from the street) the decorating features, the paint color, type of flooring, the fixtures, and make structural modifications. Building a home from scratch with a home builder will bring out your creative side as you customize your home to your taste.

**SECRET REVEALED: Building a new home is not an exact science.**

Once you have come to an agreement with the home builder on your new home price and terms, a flurry of activity begins. Your earnest money will be deposited with the builder or escrow/title company and will become part of your down payment when you close on the home. Your lender will update your loan file to make sure you are qualified for the new home price. You want to know your max qualifying loan amount so that when you go to the builder's design/decorating center, you will know how much you can add to the home and still stay within your qualifying range.

# The Builder's Lender

Every major builder has an in-house mortgage company or a list of "preferred lenders" that they will encourage you to work with. There are pros and cons to working with the builder's lender. For the builder, their in-house lender is another profit center. Mortgage loans made to their home buying clients can add thousands to their bottom line. The builder will often provide you with "incentives" for using their in-house lender like paying some or all of your closing costs. By law they can't force you to use their in-house lender but they can throw money at you to get you to want to use them. This can mean thousands of dollars in your favor if you use them. Their policy is usually that you will not get the "incentives" if you don't use the preferred lender. The problem is that in some cases the staff and loan officers at builder's lenders may not be as experienced and knowledgeable as top tier "outside lenders." I find that they can be overworked and their service level may not be as high. Top tier "outside" lenders have to compete at all levels and rise and fall on the level of their service & expertise and with their competitiveness of rates and fees. Builder's lenders tend to not be as competitive in rates and fees but they make up for it because of the "incentives." The incentive money will often make the in-house lender the best deal. However, I have witnessed where the builder's lender "absorbed" all of the incentives and charged the buyers higher rates and fees. This can happen to unsuspecting home buyers, especially first timers. It would be best to compare outside lenders' rates & fees to in-house lenders' rates and fees and make sure you get the full benefit of the builder paid incentives. Or better yet, get the builder to allow you to use the incentives with any reputable lender you choose. I will often negotiate this on behalf of my buyers so they can use any lender they want and still get the incentive money.

**SECRET REVEALED: The builder's lender is another profit center. Make sure you get the full benefit of the "incentives" offered if you use them.**

There is a benefit to you and the builder by using the in-house lender and title/escrow company. Often times they are all under one roof which allows for better flow, convenience and coordination for the transaction. If something needs to be dealt with at closing the mortgage company is across the hall, not across town. The builder has more control of the transaction as well. I like the fact that if something goes wrong during the transaction or is delayed for some reason – it is the builder's in-house people we can hold accountable. The builder can then put its foot down and demand that the mortgage or title companies get their act together. Builders don't have that leverage with "outside lenders."

**SECRET REVEALED: The builder has more control and accountability if you use their in-house services.**

# The Design Center

Within a few weeks, you will go to the design/decorating center. This is where you will customize your home. From cabinets to flooring and counter tops to light fixtures and on and on. Keep in mind that it is easy to go overboard at the design center. It is easy to spend way more than you should because it is exciting. If available, you will want your real estate professional with you to help you make wise choices. Try not to over upgrade compared to the surrounding homes in the neighborhood. If everyone in your neighborhood has the basic standard lighting package, don't buy the $2000 chandelier unless it's "really" important to you. Your real estate professional will give you input on what will help you with the re-sale of the home down the road. They know what helps or hinders the future sale so lean on their advice. Also keep in mind that the builder has incredible mark ups (profit margins) on "upgrades." You may be able to upgrade yourself after closing much cheaper than with the builder. For instance, the builder may charge $3500 to put in wood floors in the dining room whereas you could get those same wood floors put in for half of what the builder charges <u>after</u> closing. You can save a lot by doing some upgrades after market. On the other hand, it is nice to have the home completed and warranted by the builder when you move-in. Although you can save money by doing upgrades after closing, make sure it makes sense. You can't easily add a fireplace after market, so if you want one, have it put in by the builder. When you add upgrades to a home with the builder, the price of the upgrades are added to the sales price and therefore financed along with the home. Although you can save a lot of money by doing upgrading afterward, you will usually be paying cash for the upgrades after market. If you have the builder put in $10,000 in upgrades it is financed into the home and would then run about $80 per month. Most first timers need up front cash for other things so financing upgrades may be the only way to get them done.

**SECRET REVEALED: Builder upgrades are huge profit centers – don't go overboard with upgrades.**

## Construction is Stop & Go

Once your financing is moving forward and your design & decorating is completed, the builder will begin the building process. At first, you may not see anything happen on your lot for thirty to forty-five days. This is the time when the builder is finalizing plans, applying for permits, and lining up subcontractors. You may have a pre-construction meeting with your building superintendent and go over the plans and the placement on the lot. Then a week or two after that, the construction begins. Construction happens in fits and starts. There will be a lot of activity and then the construction stops. This is not a cause for alarm. City inspectors will inspect the home as it is being built. For instance, when the home is framed up, the builder cannot move forward until the city or county inspectors sign off on the framing. After inspection, the plumbers, electricians and drywallers can commence working until the next inspection.

## Visiting Your Home During Construction

As the home is being built, I suggest you visit it during construction. There are always things that are in need of adjustment. Most of the time the superintendent knows about the glitches, sometimes they don't. My suggestion is to make a list of items you notice that are wrong and give it to you to your on-site sales agent. Keep a copy of your notes. Your sales agent will go over the list with the superintendent. If you have a list of ten things you notice wrong, your superintendent will usually know nine out of ten items but that tenth item he may have overlooked. You know what plan changes and upgrades you put in your home and making lists and giving it to the on-site agent will help your builder. Whatever you do, don't try to talk directly with the workers about fixing things and don't fix them yourself. Remember, building is not an exact science. Things break, items are out of place, etc. You are buying a finished product and the builder will fix the problems. Knowing this advice will help you to not lose sleep at night. Also, be careful around construction sites to make sure that you and your children are safe.

**SECRET REVEALED: You are buying a finished product – let the builder build.**

## Inspections and Repairs – New Homes

It is recommended that you get an inspection on a new home. This will be done around the time of your final walkthroughs. Your inspector will want to wait until the home is complete and all utilities are turned on before doing the inspection. You do not want to wait until the very last minute before closing to do an inspection. You want to give the builder time to address issues and fix them prior to closing. You may consider a staged inspection. This is where the inspector will check the home out during the different stages of construction. Staged inspections cost more so you will have to weigh the value vs. cost. Remember, new homes get inspected during construction by the city or county inspectors so there is some measure of accountability with them as well. Also, your home will be warranted for one to ten years for most of the major structural systems.

**SECRET REVEALED: Your new home will be warranted for one to ten years.**

## New Home Walkthrough & Punch List

Once your new home is complete you will do a walkthrough and orientation several days before closing. You will meet the superintendent or a warranty manager and they will give you a tour of your home. They will explain all the functions of your home and how to operate all the appliances and mechanical devices. This is also the time where you will be able to make a final punch list of all remaining items yet to be completed. It is not uncommon to have a light fixture not working or a broken window needing replacing. This is also the time you will "tag" the house for minor and major cosmetic or structural deficiencies. Most of the time, the "punch" items are minor paint and drywall glitches and scratches here and there.

These will be tagged with your tape and a paint & touch up crew will come behind you and fix those items. Occasionally the repairs are big ones like a wall out of place or a sagging roofline. Keep in mind the builder will fix them but you will need to let them know. Builders can do amazing things to get a home finished on time.

## Be Firm With Final Touches

I once had a client who was having a home built with red brick and white mortar. The day they installed the brick it had rained and the white mortar turned pink. My client was upset so we called the builder to fix it. The superintendent couldn't do anything about it so we called his boss, the project manager who said he could not change the mortar color. So I went up the corporate ladder to the V.P. of construction. He came out to the home and tried to convince my buyer that it was "within tolerances." Not to my buyer! She said, "fix it or I'm not buying it." The V.P. ended up authorizing that all the brick on the front of the home be pulled off and new brick and mortar put up. I was able to pull this off because as a respected real estate professional I had a good relationship with the builder's management team. It would never have been fixed without my influence. One of the biggest leverage tools you have for getting it done right is letting the builder know that you are not closing until it is done. However, you need to be reasonable too. I have seen cases where "my" buyer went overboard and was out of line with some requests and I had to inform him that the builder was finished with the home and it was time to close. Just prior to closing, you will then have a final *final* walkthrough to make sure all of the items on the previous walkthrough were completed. I am really picky about my clients' new home being completed without scratches, dings, and glitches. You wouldn't buy a new car with dings on it. You shouldn't have to close on a new home with nicks and scratches on it. Superintendents will try to get you to overlook things or say that glitches are "within tolerance." If they are obvious – they are not within tolerance. Remember, once you sign off on the home, the builder is not going to fix dings and scratches. They will warrant the house for one to ten years after closing but cosmetics will be up to you. At the final walkthrough, you will sign off on the house as finished and acceptable to you.

**SECRET REVEALED: You can be very picky on final walkthroughs.**

Watch Video
http://bit.ly/Klvwml

## Secrets Revealed Recap

1. You can get a great deal on a home when builders are trying to "meet the numbers."

2. Builder spec homes (inventory homes) can be a great deal.

3. Builders treat buyers better if they have an agent.

4. Builders won't discount a home by the commission amount if you don't have an agent.

5. On-site sales agents do not make the final pricing decision on a home.

6. Almost all builders negotiate price & terms.

7. The best time to buy is during the beginning and the end of a phase.

8. Check out previous phases to see how the neighborhood is "holding up."

9. Don't fall in love with "model home" decorating and upgrades.

10. Building a new home is not an exact science.

11. The builder's lender is another profit center. Make sure you get the full benefit of the "incentives" offered if you use them.

12. The builder has more control and accountability if you use their in-house services.

13. Builder upgrades are huge profit centers – don't go overboard with upgrades.

14. You are buying a finished product – let the builder build.

15. Your new home will be warranted for one to ten years.

16. You can be very picky on final walkthroughs.

# Chapter 9

## Foreclosure, Short Sale and REO Secrets Revealed

Today's real estate market offers a multitude of opportunities to capitalize on the over exuberance of past years. There are tens of thousands of homes that have been foreclosed upon or are headed towards that possibility. These homes can be a great opportunity in the market but you are wise to consult with your real estate professional regarding the "realities" of these opportunities. Although foreclosures and short sales have gained a lot of media attention lately, the reality is that the good and great deals are farther and fewer between than you may have been led to believe. I would ask first time home buyers to proceed with caution and get professional advice when approaching this segment of the market.

Let's review the foreclosure process and suggest some of the more "viable" possibilities where first timers have a better chance at finding a winner in the foreclosure market.

# Pre-Foreclosure

When a home owner starts to have financial difficulties, the owners will usually start to get behind on their unsecured (credit card) debt. There are a multitude of reasons why people get behind. Job loss, medical problems, marital problems, etc. They let their credit cards go delinquent first but usually try to keep up on the house payment. When they get in further distress, they start to get behind on the house payment. They may put the home on the market and, hopefully it will sell. This is called a "distressed sale," the seller is in trouble. Once the owner gets two to three months behind on payments, they now enter into the "pre-foreclosure" stage. You may be able to get a great deal on the home, save the seller from losing the home and even put some money in their pocket. This is a viable time to help them if they have sufficient equity. This is the time before they have been served a foreclosure notice from their bank but are not making the payments. However, financial troubles can lead to the "deer-in-the-headlights look" for the distressed seller and they can find it hard to make decisions. This is the time when many owners will approach their mortgage company and discuss options. Of course, the mortgage company prefers that the owner just get caught up on payments or pay them off. If the owner can't get caught up, they may discuss a "short sale."

**SECRET REVEALED: A pre-foreclosure purchase can be a win-win for all involved.**

# Short Sales

If an owner has a lot of equity, they can usually avoid foreclosure by just reducing the price enough to garner a quick sale. The problem comes when the loan amount is too high compared to the value. The owner is "upside down" meaning they owe more than it will take to cover the expenses of the sale after loan payoff and other selling expenses. They will approach the bank and attempt to do a "short sale." This is where the bank will take less than what is owed so that it can be sold at a reasonable price on the open market. The owner agrees to market the property with a real estate professional and the bank agrees to consider offers that are "short." In theory, it is supposed to be good for the owner (by saving their credit) and the bank (by not having to go through foreclosure). In reality, a short sale does not really save the owner's credit that much. A short sale can have the same negative effect on the credit score as a foreclosure. For the bank, a short sale might help them if they can get the home sold, but if not, the bank will have to foreclose anyway. For a home buyer, there are major drawbacks in attempting to purchase a short sale. First, you are dealing with a distressed seller who is not making any money on their home. It is emotional for the seller and can be a bitter pill to swallow. The biggest problem is the lack of response from the banks that hold the mortgage. In a normal buyer/seller transaction, when you find a home you can make an offer and get a response to your offer relatively quickly. If you can come to terms – great – but if not, you can move on to another home. With a short sale, the bank has to "approve" the offer. At the time of this writing, a "short sale" response to a buyer's offer can be two to four months. This is a big problem. Buyers who are looking for a home don't want to wait months to get a response on an offer. Who wants to live in limbo hoping the bank will ever get to your offer? The reality is the banks do not have enough staff or systems set up to handle the volume of short sales. The bank clerk in charge of looking at your offer may have 150 to 200 other files to deal with. Needless to say, this can be very frustrating for all involved. Smart real estate professionals educate their buying clients about this problem and often times the decision is made to "pass" on looking at short sales. I am sure that as the volume of short sales thins out, they will become more workable, but at this time I don't find them to be a very "viable" option for first timers looking to move in a timely manner.

**SECRET REVEALED: It may take two to four months to get an answer on your short sale offer.**

# Foreclosures – The Court House Steps

If the house does not sell pre-foreclosure or short sale, the house will be sold at auction on the courthouse steps. At the court house, their will be an opening price, usually the amount to cover the bank balance and accrued expenses. The house will be bid on by potential buyers until there is a final bid – going once, going twice, sold. In 95% of the cases, the bank is the highest bidder because the auction price is higher than what the other bidders are willing to offer. If an auction bidder is successful in having the highest bid, they are required to pay cash (cashier's checks) for the property immediately. Successful bidders buy the home "as is," with no warranty and no title insurance. The reality is that there are few good deals at auctions and the bank usually is the highest bidder. Those lucky enough to get a great deal will have to pay "cash." Not a very "viable" option for a first time home buyer. So, unless you have a boat load of cash and a lot of time to research the houses offered at auction ahead of time, forget the foreclosure auctions.

**SECRET REVEALED: You have to pay cash on the barrel at foreclosure sales.**

# REO's (Real Estate Owned)

REO's are houses that have been taken back by the bank through foreclosure. If no bidder purchases the home at the auction, the bank will be the winning bidder. They will assign the house to the "REO" department. REO stands for "Real Estate Owned." The REO department will assess the home, appraise it, hire a real estate professional to market it. The bank may or may not fix the house up. It is case by case.

Bank REO's are motivated sellers. They don't want to keep the home for long and will try to liquidate to recoup losses. The bank wants the most money they can get for the home but they also don't want to keep it on the "books." For a buyer, the advantages of buying repos is that you will be able to get a quicker response from the bank than a short sale. You won't have to pay cash like you would at the foreclosure steps and you will get the title insurance and a chance to get inspections performed and to negotiate repairs. Of all the categories in the distressed property realm, I like REO's the best. You are dealing with a bank who has staff and procedures that allow for more reasonable responses and time frames. I find REO's to be a "viable" possibility for first timers.

**SECRET REVEALED: REO's are a viable option for first time homebuyers.**

# H.U.D. Homes

H.U.D. homes are foreclosed houses that were insured by F.H.A. – The Federal Housing Administration. These houses are similar to REO's in that they are already "taken back" by H.U.D. You will get title insurance (clear title). H.U.D. houses can be a good deal – but not always. You will still need the guidance of your real estate professional to determine if it is a good deal. It is purchased "as is" so you don't get the benefit of inspections and repair requests. They can be purchased for as little as $100 down. H.U.D. homes are purchased through a bidding process. Your real estate professional can show you the homes available and you can "bid" on them. This is done online once or twice a week. H.U.D. will look at all the offers and decide which is best. They will accept or decline the bids depending on H.U.D.'s "bottom line." One major difference between the foreclosure steps and H.U.D. homes is that the H.U.D. allows a home buyer time to obtain financing. You don't have to have a suitcase full of cash to buy a H.U.D. home. One problem in the auction process on H.U.D. homes is that "it's a bidding process." Buyers will sometimes bid up the price of a H.U.D. home more than what it's worth. Don't get caught up in the bidding wars on a H.U.D. home unless it is the only home for you. Often times, there is a better home at a better price just down the street.

**SECRET REVEALED: H.U.D. homes can be purchased with $100 down.**

All in all there are good opportunities in "distress sales" but do not put blinders on as there can be even better opportunities that will meet your objectives and get you in to an even better home if you weigh "all" options. Your real estate professional will help you sort through these possibilities and hopefully get you the home that is "right" for you.

Watch Video
http://bit.ly/MAjWQy

# Secrets Revealed Recap

1. A pre-foreclosure purchase can be a win-win for all involved.

2. It may take two to four months to get an answer on your short sale offer.

3. You have to pay cash on the barrel at foreclosure sales.

4. REO's are a viable option for first time homebuyers.

5. H.U.D. homes can be purchased with $100 down.

# Chapter 10

## 160 Home Buying Secrets Revealed

1. There are only a few places you can store wealth and real estate (including your home) is one of them.

2. Renters make landlords rich because of tax breaks, equity build up and loan principle buy-down. These are all the same reasons why you should consider ownership rather than renting.

3. Uncovering sources of funds to purchase a home is like a treasure hunt. The funds are everywhere you just have to find them.

4. Banks and mortgage companies need to lend money – it's their business. To stay in business they need to lend money to home buyers like you.

5. You can get your score for free and you can manipulate your score if you know what to do and what not to do.

6. Top real estate professionals save you a ton of time, effort and money and can put you in a much better negotiating position that "going it alone."

7. A buyer's agent can get you the best deal on the right home and their services don't cost you a dime.

8. Top internet real estate websites are run by tech-savvy pros but not necessarily the best qualified real estate professionals. The best agents are found by referral.

9.  Internet mortgage websites give you information but not the wisdom and service you need. The best lending pros are found by referral.
10. You don't have to let a lease keep you from buying the right home. There are win-win strategies you can use to "tell your landlord goodbye."
11. Real estate markets are cyclical.
12. Buying your first home may seem like an enormous endeavor, but it's really not.
13. Credit glitches are common and can be overcome.
14. Even today, mortgages are easier to obtain than most people think.
15. Every home buyer will experience buyer's remorse at least once during the process and must push through it.
16. The day you own a home for the first time is exhilarating.
17. Buying a first home can be a great investment.
18. A free and clear home can make retirement much easier.
19. A free and clear first home can be a great investment or vacation home.
20. First time home buying seminars are a great way to learn the process and meet real estate professionals.
21. Connect with knowledgeable real estate professionals with experience and who love what they do.
22. Keeping your first home may be your best retirement home.
23. Don't get your wisdom from the news media.
24. Buy in a buyer's market.
25. Because home payments are tax deductible, the government is partially subsidizing your home payment.
26. When interest rates go up, the value of assets (homes) usually follow.
27. Perfect opportunities are rare.
28. Owning your own home is more than just physical shelter, it can be financial shelter, an income tax shelter and a retirement expense shelter.
29. Buying a home as college housing can be a great move.
30. Buying your first home is challenging and exhilarating.
31. Your fixed rate home loan payments will someday be paid off.

32. Buying the home you are renting can be a great way to become a home owner.

33. Home owners are in more control of their housing situations.

34. A home payment can be less than rent.

35. Uncle Sam favors home ownership.

36. You can ask your employer to withhold less from your paycheck after you buy a home.

37. There can be huge tax deductions when you purchase.

38. You can enjoy up to $500,000 tax-free profit on the sale of your home.

39. More people have become wealthy by owning real estate than by other investments.

40. You can still buy a home with no money down!

41. One free and clear home can make retirement much easier.

42. Most everyone wishes they had kept their first home – myself included – hindsight is 20/20!

43. While one free and clear home can make life easier, ten free and clear homes can make you wealthy.

44. As a first time home buyer, you can easily build a team of professionals who work exclusively for you.

45. T.E.A.M. stands for Trusted Experts, Advisors, & Mentors.

46. Integrity is the foundation of trusted relationships.

47. Ask for and expect care, communication & competency.

48. True professionals seek to turn their clients into raving fans.

49. If at all possible, refer and be referred.

50. Make homeownership a goal, commit, take action, and never give up.

51. Visualize yourself in your own "dream" home.

52. Real estate is still a people and relationship business.

53. Stay away from nay sayers who don't own their own home.

54. Make a plan to become "ready, willing, and able."

55. Self-analyze what is really important in your preferred living situation.

56. A needs and wants list will help clarify objectives.

57.    If you are buying a resale home, start 90+ days before you want to move.

58.    If you plan to build, start the process nine months before you plan to move.

59.    Don't let a lease stand in the way of you buying a home.

60.    Consider buying your second home first.

61.    Get excited, then hire trusted advisors.

62.    The real estate broker/agent and lender will coordinate 90% of home buying activities.

63.    There are real estate professional who are "experts." Find them and employ them.

64.    For better or worse, 68% of home buyers work with the first agent they meet – regardless of their experience or qualifications.

65.    You have the right to your own representation and the seller/builder pays for it.

66.    Onsite builder representatives won't tell you all the hidden incentives available to you.

67.    Your agents "reputation" may help you get a better deal.

68.    Your real estate professional is your "advocate."

69.    Find a loan expert not an interest rate.

70.    Your lender is a key professional in your home buying process – choose wisely.

71.    The "New" Good Faith Estimate will help you compare lender charges.

72.    The more complete your information is up front the quicker and easier it will be to get a loan approval.

73.    You can still purchase a home with as little as 0-3.5% – total move-in.

74.    A pre-approval letter from a reputable lender can make the difference whether your offer is accepted over another.

75.    Keep in close contact with your lender when making any financial or employment moves.

76.    A fully approved loan is like having a suitcase full of cash ready to purchase any home that meets your parameters.

77.    Information about homes on the internet is incomplete at best.

78. "Sold" data is not readily available on the internet.
79. The internet can be a good source of information but not a good source of wisdom.
80. New homes are warranted for one to ten years.
81. Don't go overboard at the decorating center.
82. Resale homes are "broken in" and have more mature foliage.
83. Earnest money shows the seller you are serious.
84. Be prepared for some up front expenses before you buy a home.
85. Do "drive bys" to help eliminate homes and areas.
86. Electronic home access is much more convenient and time saving.
87. Even in a buyer's market, the good homes sell first.
88. Be aware – you can't choose your neighbors or change traffic patterns.
89. Schools and school districts have a direct impact on value and desirability.
90. Buyer's Agents will get better and more complete information than a buyer would.
91. Real estate professionals are not qualified to give tax or legal advice. Seek proper counsel.
92. Sometimes full price is the best price.
93. Make sure your agent is a negotiation "artist."
94. Your agent's "reputation" can help you or hurt you.
95. Watch out for "buyer's remorse" – it can cost you your home.
96. Your option period gives you the right to back out at little or no cost.
97. Cooperate with requests from your real estate professional and lender.
98. Buy the house before you buy the car.
99. Don't buy a home without having it inspected.
100. Try to attend the inspection. You will learn a lot about your home.
101. In an inspection report, three to thirty items "needing repair" is common.
102. Try not to schedule a move on the same day of closing.

103.  Bring to closing your ID, cashier's check, checkbook, and your spouse.
104.  Try not to close on the last day of the month.
105.  Do not apply for new credit until after closing.
106.  If you want to read all the documents, get them a few days ahead of time to review.
107.  There are almost always minor (and sometimes major) adjustments to the closing statement.
108.  You will skip your first month's payment
109.  There are many tax-deductible items on your closing statement including taxes and interest.
110.  Change your locks & security alarm codes after closing.
111.  A referral from a satisfied client is the best compliment a professional can receive.
112.  In the home loan world, credit scores are king.
113.  Mortgage lenders use the middle score of the three major credit bureaus.
114.  Establish credit with a secured credit card or credit line.
115.  Don't close credit card accounts that have been open for a long time.
116.  Paying off old collection accounts can hurt your score.
117.  Mortgage companies working with local credit bureaus can be a great help.
118.  Disputes can help correct or delete derogatory credit entries.
119.  Simple corrections can raise your score.
120.  Getting derogatory accounts deleted is like the event never happened.
121.  Multiple inquiries in a thirty-day period in the same industry has a very minor effect on the score.
122.  Keep credit card balances under 19% of the credit limit.
123.  Watch out for your credit card companies lowering your credit limit.
124.  Optimize your credit with the proper mix of accounts.
125.  Be very careful about using so-called credit counseling services and credit repair companies.
126.  Guidelines change often – work with a mortgage expert.
127.  Buyers with a job, a small down payment, and reasonably good credit can get a loan.

128. The majority of home sales in America are to first time home buyers.
129. Having the seller pay closing costs can cut the cash needed to close in half.
130. Most home loans are backed by the federal government.
131. Portfolio loans can be found at local banks and credit unions.
132. Subprime loans are all but gone (for good reason).
133. You may have a relative who will loan you the funds to buy a home.
134. Follow the ten and thirty year treasury bond yield to help determine where rates are headed.
135. Have your lender run your loan file "through the system" – (computerized underwriter).
136. Salaried buyers are qualified on gross income. Self employed are qualified on the "net."
137. Buy the home before you become self-employed.
138. F.H.A. allows for non-occupant co-signers, which is perfect for college student home buyers.
139. The builder, seller, lender, and even the real estate agent can contribute to a buyer's "cash to close."
140. You can get a great deal on a home when builders are trying to "meet the numbers."
141. Builder spec homes (inventory homes) can be a great deal.
142. Builders treat buyers better if they have an agent.
143. Builders won't discount a home by the commission amount if you don't have an agent.
144. On-site sales agents do not make the final pricing decision on a home.
145. Almost all builders negotiate price & terms.
146. The best time to buy is during the beginning and the end of a phase.
147. Check out previous phases to see how the neighborhood is "holding up."
148. Don't fall in love with "model home" decorating and upgrades.
149. Building a new home is not an exact science.

150. The builder's lender is another profit center. Make sure you get the full benefit of the "incentives" offered if you use them.

151. The builder has more control and accountability if you use their in-house services.

152. Builder upgrades are huge profit centers – don't go overboard with upgrades.

153. You are buying a finished product – let the builder build.

154. Your new home will be warranted for one to ten years.

155. You can be very picky on final walkthroughs.

156. A pre-foreclosure purchase can be a win-win for all involved.

157. It may take two to four months to get an answer on your short sale offer.

158. You have to pay cash on the barrel at foreclosure sales.

159. REO's are a viable option for first time homebuyers.

160. H.U.D. homes can be purchased with $100 down.

# **About The Author**

Kenn Renner is a nationally recognized real estate expert and speaker. He purchased his first home in 1983 at the age 19. The experience led him into the real estate and finance profession. He has devoted his entire professional career to helping clients buy and sell real estate. Since 1983 Kenn has sold more than $250,000,000 in real estate working with more than two thousand buyers and sellers. He personally has bought and sold more than one hundred houses.

Kenn produced his first seminar series "The American Dream Seminars" in 1994. He wrote his first popular booklet entitled "The Little Black Book of Home Buying Secrets" in 1996. He attributes a majority of his sales to his *live seminars* where he educates home buyers and investors how to buy and sell real estate. Since then he has produced and presented dozens of presentations that have expanded beyond real estate into goal setting, time management and business strategies, including video marketing

Kenn has appeared on national television and is a frequent guest expert on local and nationally syndicated business talk radio. He has been featured on three episodes of HGTV's #1 Rated Show "House Hunters". Kenn's episodes have been re-aired more than thirty times reaching two million viewers each time.

Kenn resides in Austin, Texas with his wife Michele and his three children, Justin, Christine and Julia. Kenn is a singer songwriter and enjoys producing and performing music in his time away from the business. He loves to travel with the family and enjoys water & winter sports and most of all - time spent with his family.

Kenn has produced over 600 videos and has the #1 real estate video channel in *the Nation with over nine million views* (YouTube.com/RennerRealty). He teaches video marketing to a nationwide audiene of Realtors and small business owners. He is a state licensed instructor for continuing education.

## Many Thanks too...

There are so many people who helped me and encouraged me to get this first book published that I would like to thank. If I missed anyone please forgive me and you have my thanks anyway. Thanks to all my current and former home buying clients – all two thousand of you! My wife Michele, George & Faye Walter and the rest of the Walter family, Daniel Sanford, Stephanie McCord, Shelly McLaughlin, Tracy Seeber, Phyllis Blackwell, Bonnie Stamos, Cindy Rapsinski, Rob Hutton, Daisy McClester, Joshua & Tiffany Geary, Scott Carley, Ras & Bev Robinson, Eddie Smith, Mary Lynne Gibbs, Jay Papasan, Dianna Kokoszka, J.P. Lewis, Ben Kinney & all the rest at the Keller Williams network & most of all Jesus.

# Additional Powerful Resources

# Speaker

Kenn Renner is a nationally recognized speaker on the subject of real estate, finance, and achievement. He has shared the podium with Michael Gerber, Tamara Lowe, Al Lowry, Rick Joyner, and many others. If you need a speaker for your event or conference, contact Kenn today! Visit www.KennRenner.Com – get to know Kenn and his professional offers and personal perspectives.

# Author

Kenn's first nationally distributed book is Home Buying Secrets Revealed – visit www.HomeBuyingSecretsRevealed.Com.

Kenn's second national release is "Power Goals: Twelve Proven Steps to Make Your Dreams Come True." Check it out at www.PowerGoalsBook.Com.

# Seminars

Kenn has produced a series of popular seminars with topics ranging from real estate & finance to goal setting and time management. You can learn more about Kenn's seminars and his speakering schedule at www.KennRenner.Com.

# Real Estate & Coaching

Kenn's flagship website www.BuyAustin.Com is a great real estate resource full of video and unique quality business content. Get personal real estate coaching from Kenn, whether you are a home buyer or seller, an investor, or a real estate professional seeking a career boost.

# YouTube Expert

Kenn has the #1 YouTube video channel in the Nation with over 9 million views. He teaches video marketing to thousands of professionals nationwide. Visit his YouTube channel – YouTube.com/RennerRealty

# Moving Assistance

Visit www.MoveAssistancePrograms.Com for great information on making your move easier, including information on financial assistance, move-up programs, lease buyouts, and guaranteed buyouts.

# Refer and Be Referred

Kenn wants to find the absolute best real estate professional for you to help you through the process of buying or investing. Being referred as a homebuyer carries a higher level of accountability and respect from a real estate professional. Much like when a doctor refers you to a specialist – you being referred to another real estate professional by Kenn carries a high level of respect. Kenn will find you the real estate professional with the highest level of care, communication and competency. Call or text 512-423-5626 for more information.

| | |
|---|---|
| Speaking: | www.KennRenner.Com |
| | www.BuyAustin.com |
| Authorship: | www.HomeBuyingSecretsRevealed.Com |
| | www.PowerGoalsBook.Com |
| Seminars: | www.KennRenner.Com |
| Coaching: | www.KennRenner.Com |
| Moving Assistance: | www.MoveAssistancePrograms.Com |
| Be Referred: | Call / Text Kenn – 512-423-5626 |

## Contact Info:

Kenn Renner
4311 Rum Runner Road
Austin, TX 78734

512-423-5626 – Call / Text
512-218-1202 – Office
512-388-1173 – Fax
Email: Kenn@BuyAustin.Com

## Earn Up to $250 for Reading This Book

That's right! I am so sure that you will find this book invaluable to you when buying your first home that I will offer you $250 from my real estate commission if you use me as your chosen real estate professional. The reason I am willing to offer this to my home buying clients is that I find that an educated buyer is much more prepared to move through the process of buying a home. This book is designed to motivate and educate you, and motivation and education saves me time and money so I pass the savings on to you. All you have to do to receive the $250 is hire me, Kenn Renner as your chosen real estate broker OR have me refer you to the best real estate professional in your area. www.HomeBuyingSecretsRevealed.Com

## Your Referral Broker

If you are not within my professional service area, I can still help you find the best real estate professional in your area. I have access to what I call the "top Tier" agents across the nation. My Top Tier agents are professional and have years of experience. They have the highest level of service, expertise and integrity. They are experts in their field. Since they value my referral they are glad to give me a small percentage of their sales commission AND they will agre to pay you $250 as well at closing. For more information on my referral program, visit www.HomeBuyingSecretsRevealed.Com

Of course to receive your referral fee, you and your real estate professional must comply with R.E.S.P.A. guidelines and all applicable local, state and federal laws. You must register with and be referred in writing by Renner Realty, Inc. to your real estate professional and Renner Realty, Inc. must have actually received the referral fee from the closing of the transaction. The referral fee must appear on the H.U.d. 1 closing statement. There must be full disclosure to all parties involved in the transaction and it must be agreed to and allowed by those parties. If unallowed, the fee cannot be paid and you will not be entitled to the referral fee.

## 100% Money Back Guarantee

I am so sure that you will benefit from the wisdom in this book that if you are not completely satisfied with what you learn, I will gladly refund you the cost of this book – no questions asked (not including taxes, and shipping and handling). If not 1000% delighted with it, just send the book back to me with your proof of purchase and I will gladly refund you the $12.95 you paid.

## Questions or Comments

Kenn Renner, Broker / Author / Speaker
Kenn@BuyAustin.Com
(512) 218-1202
www.KennRenner.Com

For more details and information, visit
www.HomeBuyingSecretsRevealed.Com

# KennRenner.Com

## Do you need a speaker?

Do you want Kenn Renner to speak to your group or event? Then content him at: (512) 218-1202 or email Kenn@BuyAustin.Com

Wether you want to purchase bulk copies of Home Buying Secrets Revealed or buy another book for a friend, get it now at www.HomeBuyingSecretsRevealed.Com.

**If you have a book that you would like to publish**, call (512) 218-1202.